Praise for
Leading Projects with Data

"Recently, Gartner claimed that 80% of today's project management tasks will be eliminated by 2030 as Artificial Intelligence takes over. On the other hand, the project economy claims that the future of work is about projects. How will this impact the fate of project management? Developing data analysis competencies will certainly play an essential role. In his book, *Leading Projects with Data*, Marcus Glowasz brings a compelling new perspective. He confirms that data-driven approaches will give us more transparency and a better understanding of the project portfolio. But he also proposes a purpose- and knowledge-driven approach to establish the right behaviors and mindset in the teams to increase project success with the use of data-informed practices. If you are a project leader or eager to learn about the future of project management, I highly recommend reading his book."

Antonio Nieto-Rodriguez, author of *HBR Project Management Handbook*, Founder Projects & Co, PMI Fellow & Past Chair

"Marcus Glowasz's *Leading Projects with Data* offers valuable perspectives on the central role that data plays in innovation and project management. His discussion of the rise of data and analytics, and the important need to deliver true business value are at the heart of this instructive and very readable book. Recommended for data and analytics leaders seeking to leverage data to improve project delivery practices and achieve positive business outcomes."

Randy Bean, author of *Fail Fast, Learn Faster: Lessons in Data-Driven Leadership*, and Founder/CEO of NewVantage Partners

"*Leading Projects with Data* focuses not only on using data and analytics to improve project performance but also on the psychological, cultural, and behavioral changes that must be implemented. This approach ensures we transition to a supportive culture and collaborative mindset rather than just the technology itself.

Many experts emphasize that the primary problem with technology is not the technology itself but rather the human-related hurdles to adapt to and benefit from it. I am confident that Mr. Glowasz's book will significantly impact anyone looking to leverage data, analytics, and technology to produce better projects."

Ricardo Viana Vargas, Ph.D., former President of the Project Management Institute, former United Nations Director of Infrastructure and Project Management

"This is a fantastic book within the world of data literacy and one that I feel non-data professionals can truly value from, as well as data professionals, but from different perspectives. Non-data professionals may not know how to bring data into a project but may have strong project management skills, and data professionals may not know how to lead projects. This book is a gem, allowing the reader and individuals to recenter and refocus their work, to bring projects to life and utilize data to do so. It is must-have reading for data-driven people, teams, and organizations."

Jordan Morrow, head of Data and Analytics at BrainStorm, author of *Be Data Literate* and *Be Data Driven*

"This book delivers an inspiring message about the value of project data. Marcus provides amazing insights regarding the data-informed approach to managing projects in an easy-to-read format full of stories and analogies. From concepts such as dark data to the quality of project decisions, the book presents models and research to demonstrate how using data successfully will improve project performance. Actions are identified that will help all project practitioners excel at managing their projects."

Paul Boudreau BA MBA PMP, author of
Applying AI to Project Management

"Based on his experience managing projects in the technology and financial services industries, Marcus Glowasz delivers a clarion call for the project management profession to adopt a more data-driven approach to managing projects. Marcus clearly recognizes that where the profession once was at the forefront, it now lags in its use of data to deliver value to our customers, stakeholders and fellow team members.

Leading Projects with Data is a must for any project leader wanting to use data and analytics more effectively and to move up the DIKW pyramid (data-information-knowledge-wisdom). Readers will find chapter takeaways as well as charts and graphics to aid in the journey to build data-informed project management practices at their organizations."

Bruce Gay, PMP, Senior Program Manager
and Principal Consultant, Astrevo

"Marcus is able to show new options in dealing with projects without underestimating the central element, the human being, in its importance for success. He has succeeded in creating a symbiosis of proven and tested approaches with intelligent data analysis that can help reduce uncertainty and position AI exactly where it can have the greatest effect, in helping to generate benefits."

Rüdiger Geist, Dipl. Pol., IPMA Level B, PMP, PfMP, Owner Spirit at PM GmbH, Member of Board of Directors at Syncwork Schweiz AG

"The magic of this book is that, whatever your starting point, it provides you with actionable insights. By looking at how data is a key component of any organizational culture through the lenses of purpose, knowledge and behavior, each single chapter will give you suggestions to improve the way data is used to increase the rate of success of your projects."

Fabio Turel, Top 10 Thought Leader on Thinkers360

"'Be knowledge-driven, not data-driven.' In the present age, innovation is king and key to the escalated pace of technological growth we are experiencing. Marcus Glowasz highlights the fact that the project management industry is littered with antiquated beliefs that any BoK will have a meaningful impact on project success rates – and draws light to the fact that this thinking may be the reason behind project failure rates. This enlightening book presents organisations and communities of practice with an opportunity to stop and see the gold in the endless river of projects. If we are able to develop collective intelligence characterized by diverse opinions, the alignment of different decision-maker types, and data and analytics, it may enable better judgment during project delivery. This is a wonderful book and a must read for PMO and project managers wanting to assess alternate solutions to enable an evidence driven project management capability."

Daniela Kellett MAIPM CPPD ChPP, President Australian Institute of Project Management (AIPM) Victorian Chapter Council, Principal Advisor Project Management at Yarra Trams

"It's time for a paradigm shift in project management. We can make a major improvement in the success rates of our projects! And although data is king, it is the people that must ultimately drive this needed change. This book is AWESOME! Marcus really did his homework then combined that with his real-world project management experience. He provides the insight and evidence that will change your mindset and spark your transformation journey for leading projects with data."

Rich Weller, Digital PMO Lead, MI-GSO | PCUBED

"The pace of change is dramatically increasing year after year in the world, but project management, that is the discipline that helps us to implement change through projects, has barely evolved in the last decades. Is this not a paradox? This book opens our mind, proposing us to move to a data-informed project management approach, showing us how to gather data applying different practices, data that combined with people´s expertise and skills, will help us to increase the success rate of our projects."

Ricardo Sastre Martín, Thought Leader in Project Management

"Leading Projects with Data highlights the essential element of data-informed project management—the human experience in building knowledge to enhance the performance of projects and project management. Human experience and intuition, along with data analytics, enable project workers to make better-informed decisions in complexity and uncertainty. Glowasz identifies the dimensions that enable organizations to transform to data-led projects — purpose, behavior, and knowledge. From this book, project workers and organizations will assess their ways of working to enable data and analytics to become a crucial part of project knowledge and best-value performance."

Lynn A. Keeys, Ph.D., PMP, Université Côte d'Azur, SKEMA, Paris, former President/CEO PMI South Africa Chapter

"It's always exciting when a new author effectively makes the case for improving the way we do project management. And Marcus Glowasz certainly does that in his new book, *Leading Projects with Data*. I especially enjoyed the section on finding purpose, and wholeheartedly agree with him that a sound purpose will "set free hidden energy, bind people together and foster an environment of trust, transparency, and accountability.""

Suzanne S. Davenport, PMP, CSM, MBA, author of *Herding Smart Cats: Project Management Reimagined*, Owner, Smart Projex Inc.

"Glowasz has issued an invitation to all project managers to join the "knowledge party" — to establish and leverage data-informed project management practices and to bring and apply their own hard won project management wisdom. More importantly, he outlines the behavioural and cultural challenges facing real transparency in projects and offers some resolutions to help project managers resolve such issues and deliver true value to their organization."

Gary Dakin, Program Manager, Financial Services

"The relationship between data and projects has always been an exciting aspect for me. Interestingly, many project managers have not seen the value in having access to data. Marcus makes a clear argument that the human side of the project manager is still an essential element for the delivery of required project outcomes to customers, while using data and information can be a valuable guide. I think Marcus' book will resonate with many, and I am sure it will create conversations everywhere and in many areas of our profession."

David Roulston FAIPM CPPE, Director/
Owner Tried and Tested PM Services

"Marcus authored a complex paradigm that touches many project management facets; digital transformation, agility in context to disruption, responsibility, adaptability and preparedness, while being responsive to business value proposition. The book brings an awareness of purpose, knowledge and behaviour as the greatest agents of the fundamental shift needed to promote an evolutionary culture of fostering knowledge share and collaboration across multiple project management aspects, hierarchical levels, functional and geographical boundaries. The book is a step ahead leading to a future holistic programmatic approach to management to deliver an integrated business value outcome."

Dr Rakesh Malhotra CPPD, ACT Chapter Councillor,
Australian Institute of Project Management (AIPM)

Leading Projects with Data

Leading Projects with Data

Overcome Behavioral and Cultural Barriers to Unlock the Hidden Value of Data in Projects

Marcus Glowasz

Published by Marcus Glowasz

First published in 2022 in Zurich, Switzerland

Copyright © Marcus Glowasz

https://marcusglowasz.com

The moral rights of the author have been asserted.

Edited by Jenny Magee

Designed and typeset in Australia by BookPOD

ISBN: 978-3-033-09522-9 (paperback)
ISBN: 978-3-033-09523-6 (ebook)

Contents

Figures

Preface

In 2008 I worked as an IT consultant with Fortis Bank in Belgium. At the time, it was listed as the world's twentieth largest financial services business by revenue.[1] The bank formed a consortium with Royal Bank of Scotland Group and Banco Santander to acquire the Dutch banking giant ABN AMRO in October 2007. It was the largest acquisition in banking history, with a deal value of €71.1billion.[2]

As a result of the merger, Fortis initiated thousands of projects to integrate the acquired assets, and I was one of more than six thousand people involved.[3]

Financing the deal and significant cultural constraints made the merger fail. The Global Financial Crisis (GFC) hit and various attempts at bailout did not succeed, sealing the fate of Fortis. French banking giant BNP Paribas took over the shop ending one of the most ambitious banking acquisition projects in failure.

Ironically, it was then that I decided to step into project management. Before that, I was part of many project teams in various industries, countries and continents, and witnessed many successes and failures.

But I have never experienced a failure as significant as the Fortis/ABN AMRO merger.

Being part of that triggered my curiosity. How could this happen? Could anyone have foreseen the cultural discrepancies between Fortis and ABN AMRO staff? How could we predict the impact of an event such as the GFC? And how could we be better prepared for uncertainty and the unknown?

I became fascinated with such questions. Given that today's businesses have to deal with frequent disruptions and changes in the marketplace, those questions should be at the top of an organization's agenda. This is especially true for the project management domain, considering the alarming number of project failures across industries.[4, 5, 6]

I decided to investigate the challenge of dealing with uncertainty that is increasingly difficult to manage by traditional means and led to so many project failures.

The project management domain relies heavily on information to make sound and informed decisions. Given the trend toward data-driven organizations, we must adopt data-driven ways of working.

Why are most project organizations still stuck in traditional ways of delivering projects while their counterparts, the business areas that are the project customers, are reaching new heights of performance and effectiveness, using advanced data and analytics technology? How can we lift and mature project management practices to a modern construct that takes advantage of the undeniable power of data and analytics?

In *Leading Projects with Data,* I explore the cultural and behavioral barriers that usually block this required evolution of project management. I will show how leaders and teams can overcome those hurdles to adopt innovative and data-informed project delivery practices in their organizations.

This book is not a manual for implementing and setting up data technology and analytical tools in your project organization. Rather, it serves as a guide to prepare the ground and build a cultural foundation for data and analytics to unleash its capabilities for effective project deliveries. It will help you redefine a project culture that enables true evidence-based practices in your organization.

The book is structured around the core elements that ensure data and analytics can effectively contribute to improving a project management department's capabilities.

Part One sets the stage and elaborates on the key challenges in managing and delivering projects today. **Part Two** dives into the importance of purpose in change and transformation, especially when leading teams toward data-informed project delivery practices. **Part Three** considers the different elements of knowledge that combined form a crucial asset and driver to enhance project delivery capabilities, and **Part Four** unpacks the behavioral and cultural traits that are required to effectively integrate data and analytics into the knowledge mix and enable its capabilities. **Part Five** brings it all together to highlight how purpose, knowledge and behavior contribute to people's engagement, heightened intelligence, and an improved capability to effectively deliver projects and value.

Leading Projects with Data is based on my years leading complex data-driven transformation programs in the technology and financial services domain, as well as my work with clients who I have helped to transform and future-proof their project delivery practices.

I hope this book gets you started on data-informed practices in projects. However, its primary aim is to spread awareness that data and analytics can no longer be ignored in projects and should not be seen as just another project management tool. We are at a critical turning point in the evolution of project management practice. Change is urgently needed, even if you do not yet recognize this urgency. But if you do not adapt, you will inevitably be left behind in constant and unproductive project firefights and eventual failures.

It is time to change, take action, and lead projects with data.

Marcus Glowasz
Zurich, Switzerland
November 2022

PART ONE

The Need for Innovation

"The enterprise that does not innovate inevitably ages and declines. And in a period of rapid change such as the present...the decline will be fast."

– Peter Drucker

CHAPTER ONE

The Rise of Data and Analytics

It is not news that we live in an information age. An era of exponential data growth enabled by the evolving capabilities of technology and the resulting possibilities of sharing, transferring and accessing information quickly. In such an environment, many describe information overload as the exposure to a tsunami of endless information that leaves us overwhelmed. With ongoing digitalization, we have little means of escaping the constant flood of information that should help us to take action, make informed decisions, and become more effective and efficient.

Almost everything has become a digital experience. You may have opted for a digital version of this book, bought with one click of a button and delivered instantly. Remember when shopping for a book meant traveling to the nearest bookstore or multiple stores to compare prices? Today's shopping experience is often completely different, made possible by technology and data that have disrupted many markets and industries.

Is data the new oil?

The term *"Data is the new oil"* was coined in 2006 by Clive Humby, a British mathematician.[1] Others have come up with variations, such as *"Data is the new currency"*, but the message is clear: data has gained significantly in value. It has become an asset for organizations and judging by the hype around it, data feels like the holy grail for innovation and competitive advantage. Facebook, Google, Netflix and Amazon are all examples of organizations that identified the value of data and took advantage of it. They represent a special breed of organization that serves as a goal for most companies today — the data-driven organization.

Many books and articles have been written about why data is so important for any business to stay competitive. A selection of these books is listed in Appendix A. Digital transformations are taking place in most organizations. Modern technologies and cloud systems are rolling out to take full advantage of data's increasing importance. All to produce insights we cannot generate through traditional means that help our day-to-day operations become faster and more precise. These insights practically enhance existing knowledge, help organizations improve decision-making, avoid failures, and spot traps or opportunities.

But to retrieve its true value, data needs to be processed — just like oil. In 2011, the senior vice president of Gartner, Peter Sondergaard, highlighted the importance of data analytics, saying, "Information is the oil of the 21st century and analytics is the combustion engine."[2] Data analytics is effectively the refinery for data, becoming the enabler for value from data and becoming data-driven.

The trend to become data-driven has become hype. It triggers the risk that the buzzword "data-driven" could lose its real meaning. Organizations may be tempted to adopt it simply because everybody else does it. The successful examples at Google and others are a welcome justification. We know this trend is rooted in the surge of Big Data and related technology, making it possible to store and process huge amounts of data. And with such a volume of data, the science and power of data analytics to draw conclusions leaves us with several concerns.

Data scandals, such as the events in the 2010s involving Facebook and the UK firm Cambridge Analytica, show how powerful data can be. In that case, Cambridge Analytica acquired and analyzed the personal data of eighty-seven million Facebook users in terms of people's behaviors, political preferences, general interests and motivations to model their personalities and traits.[3]

With these actions, Cambridge Analytica is believed to have influenced the outcome of US presidential elections by manipulating people's voting behavior using derived insights from analyzed user data and running targeted campaigns tailored to user profiles.[4]

On the positive side, data analytics have significantly helped to fight COVID-19 by generating predictions of the numbers of infected people in a particular geographic region, helping plan for required medical supplies and treatment, bed capacities, and the most effective allocation of medical staff.

Both examples show the rising power of data in various areas of our society. They also remind us that data and analytics need to be used consciously, carefully and thoughtfully, as their improper use could result in unintended and potentially negative effects. In the project management domain, that means data and analytics should not be misused as a tool or a methodology. A project management tool helps a project manager to automate work to some degree or facilitate specific actions. For example, Microsoft Project helps you build project schedules with less effort than a spreadsheet. Atlassian Jira digitalizes your Scrum or Kanban boards and makes boards more accessible and efficient. Similarly, methodologies like Scrum, Waterfall, SAFe (Scaled Agile Framework) and RUP (Rational Unified Process) are part of a toolset that can be used and applied depending on the type of project. You can use parts or make them hybrid, and different methods or tools can operate across project teams.

That flexibility doesn't exist where data analytics are concerned. It is a concept rather than a methodology — an approach to a new way of thinking and examining every element of a project. To make data and analytics truly valuable for the project management domain, you cannot use it here and there, whenever you feel like it, or have one team using it and others not. It is a fundamental change that should be applied consistently. Even though it can be considered basic, it should not become difficult or complex to achieve.

Numerous books, manuals and playbooks guide organizations on the best ways to get digitally fit by following best practices for digital transformation and becoming data-driven. Such literature provides general guidance on digital transformation, primarily in terms of platforms, transformation strategy, and organizational culture. As today's big data technology and related tools and platforms are relatively mature, the need for a change in company culture towards a data-driven mindset receives a lot of attention in transformation initiatives. Considering some seventy percent of companies fail to become data-driven, there is a valid concern that cultural factors are often underestimated.[5]

For a transformation to be successful, we must also consider the different layers of culture and specific behaviors within an organization. Business areas work differently and have contrasting challenges and priorities. Salespeople and backend change functions may follow the same overall interests of the organization while operating in very different ways. Accordingly, becoming data-driven means looking at the problem statements individually to ensure that transitioning to data-driven practices makes sense.

We cannot ignore data and analytics

The same is, of course, valid for project management. And it is possibly a trickier area because projects deal with so much uncertainty. Project managers must plan for future events and deal with people and their behaviors, while handling time and budget constraints. All to deliver something that likely will change in scope along the way.

But do projects need to transition to a data-driven approach? In Chapter Two, you will learn of the urgent need to improve the performance of project management and delivery to ensure that value is delivered to project customers. This is based on the increasing challenges of delivering projects on their defined targets and the resulting downward trend in project success rates.

Data and analytics have already shown that they can provide a lot of value to organizations. They help them be more competitive, efficient and prepared for a future that will be more disruptive than ever. And such change is desperately needed for the domain of project management to stop the negative trends and increasing costs of project failures.

Cultural and behavioral implications

Given the various challenges and constraints in the project management area, successful transition depends on the cultural and behavioral aspects of the people operating in projects. While many organizations and teams have an appetite to change their project management departments to a data-driven construct, many also focus primarily on how to make project data available, what technologies to use, etc.

Data does not drive things — people do.

Data and technology should not be the primary concern, although there are certainly some challenges to overcome. But what is often easily overlooked is the people factor. Becoming data-driven is a significant change. Unless people's mindset concerns are adequately addressed, it doesn't matter how much data you have, how good your data or how advanced your technology. In this sense, "data-driven" is often somewhat misleading because data does not drive things — people do.

That is why I prefer the term *data-informed* in the context of using data and analytics in the project management domain. You probably have read about how organizations want to become more data-driven and reach more data-driven decisions. And you've probably heard the term data-driven more often than data-informed.

Data-informed simply means people remain the driving force in projects, and their decisions are informed by their experience, skills and knowledge, as well as data and analytics. Data should be seen as a complementary source of information and knowledge that informs, not mandates, you as the decision-maker. I will dive deeper into this in the following chapters.

Keep in mind that this book is not a technical blueprint or guide to implementing data analytics and related technology for project management. It is not a book for data scientists, nor will I go into technical details.

Rather, the book will target the cultural and behavioral factors for a transition to data-informed project management practices. These are frequently overlooked, primarily because of general misconceptions about data and analytics, and their particular implications in project management.

Organizational culture and peoples' underlying behaviors and mindsets require a shift to enable data and analytics capabilities in the project management space.

This is a new way of thinking. It's an important and much-needed change to project management practice. This book will help you understand this new way of thinking. You'll appreciate what behaviors are impacted and what you can do to move toward effectively using data and analytics in project management.

....

The need for constant reinvention

Project management is the business of change. Projects are temporary initiatives whose goal is to change something for the better. Hence, project management is an essential discipline in today's age of frequent disruption, turbulence and fast-changing messages. Projects are becoming the lifeblood of organizations, given the constant need to adapt to new circumstances, conditions and practices. Projects deliver the required changes to drive an organization's agenda to progress and evolve.

Antonio Nieto-Rodriguez, a world-renowned thought leader in project management, argues that we will see an unprecedented increase in project work as part of what he describes as the *project economy*.[6] This term is synonymous with value-focused delivery of change through projects.

The Project Management Institute (PMI) calls the project economy a fundamental paradigm shift, as it redefines the profile of a successful project manager in response to the fast pace of evolution and change in technology.[7] The need is for an increased focus on value delivery and customer issues. It requires new skills and abilities, such as improved agility and an innovative mindset.[8] But it primarily requires a new way of thinking and a shift from a project culture to one that facilitates what Aidan McCullen refers to as *permanent reinvention* in his book *Undisruptable*.[9]

Sunil Prashara, former president and CEO of PMI, said that among the skills of project professionals must be the capability of "leveraging technology, leveraging big data to give you insights as to what your next step and decision should be."[10] That sounds great, but how can we adopt those capabilities and, most importantly, how can we maintain them going forward?

The message keeps changing

In project management, progress has been too slow in innovation and adapting to changes in the world and project environments. Massive changes over the last two decades, primarily in technology, have impacted organizations and their business models, resulting in the evolution of practices. Today, more than half the world's population has access to the internet (compared with less than seven percent in 2000), and nearly half own a smartphone (nearly double since 2016 to approximately 6.6. billion users in 2022). Electric cars have become mainstream and will soon be flying. Today we can create houses, manufacturing parts, medicines, and even human organs using a 3D printer.[11]

Such progress has helped build our ability to address major global issues.

All those significant changes were possible due to technological advances and primarily by taking advantage of the ever-increasing power of data, its value, and the insights we can derive from it. But this comes with new challenges.

In 2020, Kanni Wignaraja, United Nations assistant secretary-general and UNDP regional director for Asia and the Pacific, described six leadership lessons from COVID-19. One was that the message changes all the time. She said, "We don't know what we don't know. As new data comes in, what we know changes, sometimes dramatically. You probably have to say more often than you would like to – 'I was wrong' or 'there are new facts, and I change my views.'"[12]

The dynamics of today's environments and the rapid change in communicated messages make traditional ways of working obsolete. Adopting new skills, changing the ways of working, and redefining our operating model in projects is a great start, but they must be continuously reviewed, revalidated and refined. The profound concept of learning, unlearning and relearning is more relevant than ever. What was valid yesterday may be obsolete today. The new reality

> *What was valid yesterday may be obsolete today.*

is to constantly question the status quo and undergo an approach of permanent reinvention. As Kanni Wignaraja commented, "building the plane as we fly it" has become a new reality. And this is especially valid for the project management discipline.

With today's dynamics and the increased pace of change expected in coming years, traditional capabilities in project management have reached their limit. This explains the capability and knowledge gap evident in declining project success rates.

What's stopping us?

The ultimate question is what needs to be done to turn the ship around, get into more manageable waters and away from constant heavy storms and turbulence.

The increasing complexity and uncertainty in business environments caused project managers long ago to leave the bridges of their ships and seal the leaks while the rest of the team tried to keep the boat moving. Imagine those leaks as knowledge and information gaps in projects. Many decisions lack proper information, relying on experience and intuition. But that is not sufficient to fill all those leaks. Project managers use their experience, but missing information means such decision-making often lacks depth and a forward-looking approach. The result is that they may fill a leak but two new ones open elsewhere.

Who is steering the project ship if the project manager is constantly busy trying to seal those leaks? Too often, this misdirected effort results in a complete project failure or a mere delivery of output rather than actual valuable project outcomes.

One solution could be to hire a dedicated person to help seal the leaks, so the project manager can dedicate themselves to their primary task of navigation. This often happens, but essentially it is a band-aid on a much bigger problem. It may slow the leak temporarily, but it doesn't stop it. That's because the leak (the information gap) is steadily increasing, so throwing people or money at it is not a sustainable solution. The problem will reappear, bigger than before.

Therefore, the solution to stopping the leak is a fundamental rethinking of our approach to project management.

The solution is not to find a better way to seal the leaks. The solution is to exchange the ship for a modern version that is stable enough to respond properly to conditions. The old ship was built on experience and intuition, and while it worked fine for a while, it is now outdated and we urgently need a new one.

Some call it a paradigm shift, others a revolution, but a new ship is required, whatever the label. One that still relies heavily on experience, intelligence and intuition but has an important new feature: data.

PART ONE

Chapter takeaways

- Introducing data and analytics changes the way of managing and delivering projects but shouldn't be seen as difficult and complex to achieve.

- For the transformation to be successful, we need to consider the different layers of culture and specific behaviors within an organization. These factors are easily overlooked because of misconceptions about data and analytics.

- The dynamics of today's environments and the rapid change in communicated messages make traditional ways of working obsolete. The expression "building the plane as we fly it" has become our new reality.

CHAPTER TWO

Project Management Needs an Upgrade

Project management practice is a discipline like no other. It requires constant revision and updates based on new ways of thinking and more innovative ways to manage projects through their lifecycle, to eventually deliver business value on time, on budget and with the expected benefits. Over thousands of years, project management has undergone many changes to adapt to changing needs and increase the likelihood of successful outcomes. That means we are always seeking new techniques, tools or ways to manage projects, promising a more effective, efficient and eventually more successful way to deliver projects.

There are plenty of examples of major milestones in project management history. These include the introduction of Gantt charts in the early 1900s, the Critical Path Method (CPM) in the 1950s, and the writing of the Agile Manifesto in 2001.[1] Each of those techniques had a significant and, in some cases, revolutionary impact, as they represented significant advancement and modernization of project management techniques. They were so important that they became an essential part of project management education and related programs, classes, textbooks and certification programs. Those evolutionary steps are critical as they reflect increasing demand from project customers. Demands to projects change as business environments evolve.

Given that the discipline of project management has evolved, some practices have become obsolete because they did not establish themselves as reliable ways to manage projects, did not provide the intended effect or improvement, or simply became outdated. Even established ways of working will be replaced with emerging methodologies. We've seen this as the agile method outperformed Waterfall in terms of applied project delivery practices. Arguably, that has meant Waterfall is today usually seen as an outdated way of working, primarily in software development projects.

Project management must constantly evolve to remain relevant as a business practice. Project management associations like the Project Management Institute (PMI), International Project Management Association (IPMA), or Association for Project Management (APM) regularly publish updated bodies of knowledge with adjustments to common practices and techniques. That ensures the continual development of the project management discipline. Updates are based on applied practices and related feedback regarding their suitability. A key factor must be business and customer environments that set the targets regarding expected project benefits and value. The project management practice has the mandate to deliver projects in the most efficient (meeting the targets of budget and schedule) and effective (meeting the targets of scope, quality and benefits) ways.

....

We're lagging behind

It seems clear then that, in changing business environments, project management practices must continue to be updated and enhanced. But with increasing business dynamics and complexity and resulting frequent changes, the evolution of project management needs to increase its pace accordingly. There is a correlation between the maturity of project management practices and the level of complexity in business environments.

The frequent review of project success rates across various industries verifies the health of this correlation. While various initiatives frequently measure project outcomes, no consistent number accurately assesses how well projects perform.

In this book, you will learn of an alarming trend with projects increasingly underperforming and failing across various industry sectors. It should come as no surprise; the project management industry has long suffered from low project success rates. We know that project management associations try to update and enhance best practices with learnings from identified knowledge gaps, and feed them into project management practitioner education. Other measures have included the introduction of new methodologies specific to certain types of projects.

While there is no doubt that those measures are essential, there has been no significant breakthrough in achieving consistently high-performing projects. It feels like most efforts in advancing project management practices have succeeded only in maintaining mediocre success. Statistics and surveys to determine project success rates have not shown significant improvement since capturing the numbers began in the early 1990s. The different methods and surveys from various associations and other independent research bodies show a wide range of numbers, probably due to the debate around what project success actually means and how to measure it.[2,3,4,5] What is consistent is that there is no positive trend for project success rates to be identified, although we would usually expect this with all the effort put into advancing project management practices.

> *Project success rates are going from bad to worse.*

While we have been somewhat successful in maintaining mediocre success rates, the alarming trend shows that project success rates are decreasing and project failures are rising, especially in the case of technology projects.[6] In other words, project success rates are going from bad to worse. The amount of money lost due to failed projects is enormous and increasing.

The cost of project failures

The annual investment in projects accounts for USD 48 trillion. Considering the increasing demand for project management professionals, the annual investment in projects is on the rise.[7] Antonio Nieto-Rodriguez has written about the project economy in his latest book, the *Project Management Handbook*. He emphasizes that projects have become a crucial vehicle to create value in organizations, supporting the trend toward a significant growth of project-driven activities.[8]

But according to PMI's 2018 edition of *Pulse of the Profession*, for every billion US dollars invested in projects, 99 million are wasted due to poor project performance or failures.[9]

If we take the annual investment of USD 48 trillion, that means failed projects waste a whopping 4.752 trillion every year. We cannot ignore such high numbers, especially when organizations invest increasing amounts of money and rely more and more on successful project outcomes. Without an appropriate response to failure rates and wasted money, these expenses will continue to grow exponentially.

....

The growth in business dynamics

So, why are we seeing this trend towards increasingly failing projects? It is frequently argued that business environments are becoming more complex, volatile, uncertain and ambiguous (VUCA), resulting in different business dynamics and the need for a different approach to operating a business. The term VUCA reminds us that businesses operate at a faster pace than before. However, this natural phenomenon is the result of ongoing evolution. It is all relative.

Today it is data and digitalization that increase the speed of any transaction, whether it is processing payments, buying air tickets, approving money transfers, sharing documents or calling a business partner on the other side of the world.

A century ago, cars and telephones revolutionized day-to-day operations in organizations. Everything became faster, resulting in greater complexity and uncertainty — simply because so much was unknown. It's similar today, where we feel overwhelmed by the flood of data and information that reaches us every moment.

In other words, there is naturally an increase in business dynamics. And, given the speed, things are becoming more complex and volatile. But if they weren't, it would mean that nothing evolved, nothing changed and nothing was learned. The concept of VUCA has always been present, even though the term was only introduced in 1987 in a military context.[10] Sure, things are changing much faster today, but we also have other means to respond and adapt to complexity and uncertainty.

> *VUCA is only painful if we stop adapting to complexity.*

Unfortunately, VUCA has become a negative term, indicating suffering and pain. But VUCA is only painful if we stop adapting to complexity.

Ironically, I frequently get eye rolls when people realize I don't have the latest and greatest iPhones and I am still very happy with a seven-year-old Blackberry. Am I not evolving or riding along with the changes in complexity, creating some pain for myself? Am I old-fashioned? Maybe one of those grumpy old guys who ignores today's possibilities and lives in the past? No, not really. Besides that, it has a lot to do with personal preference. Having an older phone doesn't mean I'm not up-to-date with trends and opportunities or at eye-level with complexity. What is important is not the latest and greatest technology and following the trends, but rather understanding the demand for effectiveness and efficiency, being aware of what is available (and potentially more suitable) to meet that demand, and being open to change. That doesn't necessarily mean following any particular trend. It means looking out for anything that could help me become better at what I do. Would the latest iPhone make me more efficient in my work? No, not really. But maybe the next version might, and then I may change.

The key is openness to change and disruption, identifying changing needs and challenges, exploring suitable measures to address them and taking action.

Challenge #1: The need for faster project decisions

Change is happening fast and often, triggering a need for rapid, informed, high-quality decision-making. When forced to make quicker decisions, our cognitive limitations are exposed, with the potential to lower the quality and impact of decisions significantly. Previous strategies for decision-making improvements were primarily based on accumulated experience and expertise, learning from failed decisions, and removing bias from our judgments. Now such concepts often require more time than we have. In other words, traditional methods for decision-making have become too slow and are, therefore, too often ineffective. In a survey conducted by McKinsey, only thirty-seven percent of respondents said that their organizations' decisions were made quickly and of high quality.[11]

Good project managers know the art of selecting the right tools, processes, knowledge and resources.

As Lev Virine and Michael Trumper argue in their book *Project Decisions*, "Project management is the art of making the right decisions."[12] Good project managers know the art of selecting the right tools, processes, knowledge and resources, to make the best possible and most informed decision. Given the pace of change, business dynamics and the increasing speed at which quality decisions are expected to be made, the art of decision-making also lies in constantly reviewing how to make them better and faster. Hence, two questions need always to be reviewed:

1. How can we achieve the highest degree of informed decision-making?
2. How can we speed up our decision-making?

Remember, though, that there's no final answer to either question because what is considered fast decision-making today likely will be a slow process tomorrow. The world is always moving and will move faster tomorrow than it did today.

Challenge #2: There's too much information

The more informed we want to become, the more information needs to be available, right? Well, that's not a problem. There's more data and information out there than we can imagine. And it is growing faster than ever. In 2018, a report titled *Data Age 2025* from the International Data Corporation (IDC) predicted the growth of all globally available data by 530% between 2018 and 2025.[13] This is illustrated in figure 1.

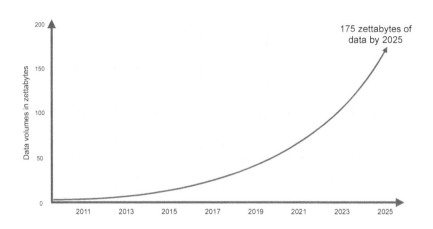

Figure 1: Predicted growth in globally available data

Indeed, there is no lack of data. But the question is how anyone could process and analyze more and more data when we have less and less time available to make decisions. This calls for a different approach to gathering data and information, analyzing the same, and generating genuine and useful insights for high-quality and fast decision-making. It means, without doubt, that the traditional approach to making project decisions is outdated and requires revision. In other words, it requires a complete overhaul and a new mindset, as we will see in the following chapters.

....

The real challenge: misaligned innovation strategies

The fast pace of technological changes, including the trend toward data-driven organizations, impacts project management and results in a strong need to change and adapt.

But the key issue of low project success rates is a growing gap between project delivery functions and their capabilities on one side, and on the other side, the receiver — the project clients and related business areas. Organizations and their business areas evolve and mature. New processes raise the bar of effectiveness and efficiency. The primary goal of digital transformations happening in most organizations is to advance and improve organizational capabilities and adapt to the rules of business environments, their actors and demands.

Amazon is preparing to deliver goods faster than ever using drone capabilities — in some cases getting items to customers in less than an hour.[14] Everything becomes faster, and with it, the demand from the receiver, the customer. If you order something online today, you expect to receive it within a couple of days. Soon, the expectation will be for same-day or even same-hour delivery. Organizations need to align with growing expectations, raising the bar of their capabilities.

Project management is in its current (and rather low-performing) state because the discipline has hardly evolved or improved over time. Think about the tools and methods that are in use. Most are decades old and haven't seen innovation. While many other areas around us are progressing, upgrading with high tech, employing intelligent technology and constantly seeking novel ideas and methods, the project management space hasn't seen parallel changes. The

> *The project management space hasn't seen parallel changes.*

growing gap between capability and maturity means a misalignment in innovation strategies. They are not synchronized, leading to a capability gap that slows overall progress and effectiveness.

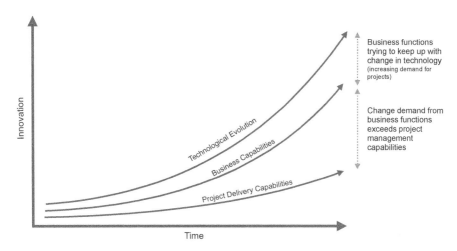

Figure 2: Increasing capability gap due to
non-synchronized innovation

I have observed this rather drastically in regulatory projects in large banks in the financial crime compliance and anti-money laundering area. Projects were initiated to deliver tools that facilitate data-driven practices, intelligent software applications powered by artificial intelligence (AI), data lakes, robotics, etc. The project client significantly ramped up their functional capabilities out of regulatory demands and the constant and increasing risk that criminals take advantage of the latest technological capabilities to find loopholes in the financial systems to run their money laundering schemes. Hence, to fight financial crime, banks have no choice but to develop a suitable defense mechanism. They are forced into continuous improvement.

And projects are crucial to delivering upgrades to compliance systems, implementing AI, machine learning, and so forth. Far from stopping, the demand is increasing alongside the pace of technological progress.

To illustrate the dilemma, think about Formula 1 racing. Each racing team tries to provide its driver with the best possible and fastest car so they can win the championship. For years, the teams Ferrari and Mercedes have fought a battle at the top. They hire the best drivers, so they need to give them the best cars. The construction teams have to deliver a car that will be faster than before and faster than the competition. Those construction teams rely on modern and advanced methods and technology to build those cars.

In many organizations, it often feels like project teams need to deliver an upgraded Ferrari with the most advanced and best engine but continue using outdated tools and instruments to make that happen. The project client drives a Ferrari while the project team uses an old Volkswagen to operate and deliver.

Project management needs to get to the same maturity level as their counterparts on the project client side. They must make continuous efforts to align and evolve and not fall back into old low-performing patterns.

From survival to excellence

Sadly many project organizations do not realize this gap and drown in survival mode, desperately trying to keep up with the overall pace. And project teams are then busier in their attempts to stop the bleeding by addressing the symptoms of a non-performing project management practice rather than fixing the root cause of the problem.

If you think that sounds too dramatic, then you are not yet feeling the pain. That is great, but I can guarantee you will face those issues sooner rather than later unless you take action now.

That means applying a new project delivery model that solves the common project delivery problems for an entire project management practice, not just an immediate issue shifting one project across the finish line. Rather than continuing to explore new and better ways to fix a leaky, sinking ship, we must replace the entire rusty hull with a new one that is fit for purpose and fit for the future. In other words, we must make project management a sustainable and reliable practice again.

Figure 3 shows the proposed steps to get out of this current dilemma and revive the evolutionary nature of project management.

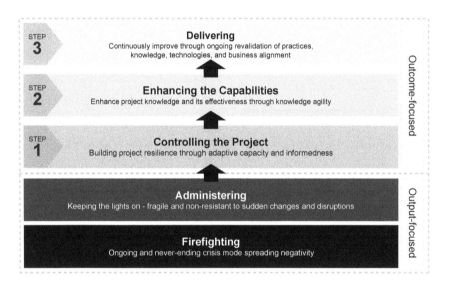

Figure 3: Steps for a transition to data-informed project management

Step 1: Controlling the project

Many project teams are effectively just surviving and constantly undergo a stretch towards project delivery. Schedules are often unrealistic, estimates way too optimistic, risks not fully captured, and unexpected and disruptive events generate massive turbulence. In short, there is a lack of control and project success becomes a lottery. Often, the resulting approach is to "get it over with" and limit efforts to protect agreed timelines and financial forecasts. In short, the main goal is to produce the output while losing sight of the intended outcome.

The primary problem with this approach is that project teams are highly vulnerable as they have no measures to respond to unexpected events. Any disruption could mean the project's failure or send the team into complete chaos. Based on the degree of uncertainty, disruption in projects is the norm, and no team should expect a smooth ride. Of course, the trained project manager knows that, and their response includes enough buffer or contingency into the project forecast to account for the unexpected. But while project managers are used to using their experience and gut feeling and often add significant time to the schedule to ensure a margin for anything unplanned, this way of delivering projects is not very efficient or reliable. In today's world, that is no longer acceptable. While uncertainty needs to be baked into project plans by adding a reasonable buffer, project managers are increasingly challenged and no longer have the freedom they used to have. Accordingly, the risk of failure grows if the project team has neither the capability nor the means to respond properly to disruption.

> *Many project teams are unaware that they are operating in a survival mode.*

Interestingly, many project teams are unaware that they are operating in a survival mode and honestly believe they are reasonably well set up. That is what led me to distinguish between the two stages in survival mode, Firefighting and Administering.

Firefighting

Firefighting usually means things are going bad, and the team is heavily in crisis mode. Of course, crises always happen, and things rarely go as planned. But you have a serious problem when firefighting becomes a constant mode. If people feel like they are stumbling from one crisis to the next, it's a clear sign that something is deeply wrong with how a project organization operates.

It happens when people and teams are constantly running on the edge, missing milestones, frequently working long hours or weekends, underdelivering or delivering projects at the last minute, and are always close to missing a critical delivery date. They have no time to breathe because the next project and crisis are already waiting. Sooner or later, they lose motivation, disengage, or even burn out.

There's a growing risk that, eventually, a deadline will be missed. With project teams entering turbulence, stress and firefighting modes increase the focus on output and decrease the emphasis on project outcomes. The value a project is supposed to produce gets diminished. Projects fail.

As they fail to deliver on project and value targets, project teams fall into the trap of embarrassment and fear. The result is an increased focus on avoiding failures in subsequent projects and deliveries, shifting them even further from

> *Project teams fall into the trap of embarrassment and fear.*

successful and valuable outcomes. To avoid failure, teams follow the primary goal of delivering their projects on time and within budget, regardless of whether such outputs provide valuable outcomes to the project stakeholders.

That turns projects into an exercise of re-establishing self-esteem and competence rather than adding value. People disengage, resulting in an increased risk of failure. In a Gallup article, Benoit Hardy-Vallée highlights that one factor contributing to project failures is the disengagement of employees and stakeholders due to a lack of attention to employees' emotions.[15]

The firefighting mode is a cycle of negativity that can grow exponentially into a sort of cancer. It requires urgent treatment as the stage is characterized by the loss of motivation, engagement, people, money and value. Eventually, it impacts overall organizational performance. It is not a sustainable way to deliver projects.

In case you are wondering, introducing data analytics to solve your firefighting problem would be like pouring petrol onto the fire that your team is desperately trying to put out. Transitioning to a data-informed practice from a firefighting mode turns on the wrong expectations. Such a transition requires focus, commitment, patience and an appropriate mindset.

Your house is on fire, and you must extinguish the flames before considering extending and modernizing it.

Administering

Many project management practices do not seem to experience wildfires and appear in reasonably decent shape. Such practices follow an established framework, have well-thought governance in place, and are also set up more flexibly by employing agile practices.

Agile is often used as the magic answer to any doubts about project performance, effectiveness, responsiveness and adaptability. "We are agile" seems to translate in many cases to "We can handle anything." That assumes Agile takes care of everything, including disruptions, turbulence, frequent and rapid changes and everything else that could be regarded a threat to project performance. That couldn't be further from today's reality. While Agile is undoubtedly a vital methodology and provides flexibility to account for today's volatility and frequently changing project requirements, it isn't enough for true project resilience.

Agile is a team's ability to respond faster to change and is used widely in uncertain and volatile environments. It is effective for redirecting and adapting to new conditions as long as there is enough time to understand how to do so. But the problem is that today's pace of change and disruption reduces this luxury of time, with less available to make a decision based on a change or a new condition.

To decide faster, people need appropriate information so they can exercise their adaptive capacity through agile methods.

That means the project may appear healthy and stable when it is actually fragile and susceptible to sudden changes and disruptions. Projects quickly end up in the turbulence that leads to project failure; a vicious circle that drives it into firefighting mode.

It is, therefore, vital to develop a true resilience that takes into account the critical factors of adaptability and informedness, to create a reasonable degree of stability that increases the chances of withstanding even the strongest storms.

Step 2: Enhancing capabilities

Establishing effective project resilience, by focusing on sharing and collaboration, and building adaptive capacity, are important first steps toward knowledge agility. The concept describes a continuous exploration and validation of new sources, techniques and methods that contribute to project knowledge. It is practically about stretching the knowledge and information muscles developed as part of becoming resilient. And that is where we dive deeper into leveraging data and analytics to enhance our project knowledge and capabilities.

Step 3: Delivering

A mature and informed project management practice should result in successful project delivery that generates real business value. But maturity must be measured by the ability of teams to consistently deliver business value and benefits. Project success should not be a rare event.

One issue is that project management is rarely updated with new and modern methods that align with the maturity of the business environments it serves. With businesses undergoing digital transformation and introducing emerging innovative technology, the project management practice needs to keep pace and evolve further.

That means maintaining and growing knowledge for better insights towards continuously informed project decisions and continuously revalidating people's behaviors, emerging tools and technologies that could help improve project delivery practices. It is primarily about constantly realigning capabilities between a project management practice and related business areas, and ensuring that project teams can keep delivering business value.

Chapter takeaways

- Despite frequent updates to bodies of knowledge by leading project management associations and the introduction of new delivery methodologies, project success rates remain consistently low, resulting in ongoing high sunk costs for organizations.

- The rapid growth in business dynamics and slow progress in innovating and evolving project delivery processes have caused an increasing gap and a misalignment between project delivery, business capabilities and technological advances. The need for faster and better project decisions requires new informed practices and taking advantage of exponentially growing information.

- Transitioning to a data-informed approach shifts teams from an output-focused mode to a high-performance and outcome-focused practice. This is done by strengthening resilience, enhancing project knowledge through knowledge agility and establishing a mindset of continuous improvement.

CHAPTER THREE

Paving the Way for Data

Before we go further with a data-informed approach to project management and delivery, let's take a moment to clarify how data and analytics relate to each other and what those terms mean.

There are many definitions of data, which we will dive deeper into in Part Three. For now, we can say that data is a representation and collection of facts or figures, and (for the scope of this book) it refers to facts that are relevant to a project and a related business problem. Analytics uses data as an input for analysis, interpretation and the identification of patterns to generate insights that otherwise could not be detected.

To make this more tangible, think about Lego. If you have ever been to Legoland and seen what can be created from Lego blocks, you must have been amazed. The blocks are like data we analyze to see how they combine to create something cool and valuable. We analyze a larger set of such data elements and use creativity and experimentation skills to find meaningful combinations and patterns. Identifying those patterns can help to describe a current business situation, understand why something happened, predict what likely will happen, or prescribe specific future actions, as figure 4 illustrates.

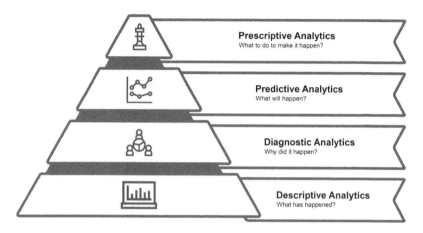

Figure 4: Types of data analytics

Hence, there is a close relationship between data and analytics, generating value. Or, in the words of Richard Benjamins, chief AI & data strategist at Telefonica, "There is no analytics without data, and data without analytics does not create value."[1]

Make data and analytics work for projects

In the context of project management, the value of data and analytics is ideal for filling existing capability gaps and lifting them to a level of project delivery effectiveness that aligns with today's business dynamics.

To fully unlock their power and value, data and analytics must contribute fully to project delivery effectiveness, optimize project management knowledge and achieve a collective intelligence, all of which is informed by human intellect, experience and data-driven insights.

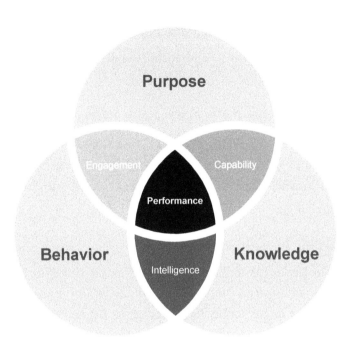

*Figure 5: Enhancing and optimizing knowledge
with data for best performance*

In the model in figure 5, the key factors of purpose, people's behavior and knowledge provide the basis for unearthing effective capabilities in a project management practice and transitioning to a data-informed project delivery model.

Parts Two, Three and Four of the book look at each of these elements in depth.

Purpose

Purpose is often confused with goals. Many people think that by setting project goals, they have automatically established a project purpose; however, this is a misconception.

While a project goal defines what a project should produce, purpose provides information about why a project exists. It is the defined purpose that gives meaning to the project. Any project should have a business justification and reason to spend money and effort for a projected change.

When setting the purpose for a project, many organizations stop there. But that means they miss the importance of aligning purpose with established project management practices and frameworks and the overarching organizational purpose and business strategies.

In Part Two, I will dive into purpose as a vehicle to deliver true business value and the resulting need to employ innovative and data-informed project delivery practices.

Knowledge

Part Three of this book explores knowledge as a key element for the intended transformation.

Value comes from the aggregation of knowledge.

Learning and knowledge gathering, of course, should never stop. Practically, we build up further knowledge with every project we conduct. Imagine a project to build a house. The processes and practices to construct buildings effectively require experience and knowledge aggregated over many years.

Accordingly, we must never stop accruing new knowledge. And we must build knowledge on top of what we already know, so we don't have to reinvent the wheel. In the end, value comes from the aggregation of knowledge. Unfortunately, this gets forgotten, and the evolution of project management stalls more often than it progresses. Evolution is not an exercise in optimizing practices, it's about advancing, innovating and making them suitable for the environments in which they are applied.

As mentioned earlier, there are plenty of inspiring quotes about data being the new oil, the new currency, or today's most valuable asset. And while I don't argue with them, we must realize that the broader element of knowledge drives the evolution of project management. That's why we apply the process of Lessons Learned

> *There is usually plenty of emphasis on acquiring knowledge and expertise and less on maintaining, exploring and enhancing it.*

or retrospectives in projects. Learning from experience eventually increases knowledge. Those practices are not becoming obsolete, but we add data and analytics to the existing contributors of experience and intuition to fill the gaps that derive from our human shortfalls.

Consequently, knowledge is the best weapon in your project toolkit to achieve delivery success; the more, the better. Unfortunately, there is usually plenty of emphasis on acquiring knowledge and expertise and less on maintaining, exploring and enhancing it. As Benjamin Franklin said, "An investment in knowledge pays the best interest."

Behavior

Investing in knowledge means exploring and adding new sources of knowledge. Data and analytics are effectively added to the knowledge mix, complementing existing knowledge from experience, intuition and expertise. But the key to fully unlocking the value of data in projects is a new mindset and thinking for project professionals. The behaviors required to effectively balance the different knowledge contributors need to drive new ways of collaborating across boundaries and generate a new project culture of constantly exploring the new and unknown in the pursuit of continuous improvement.

In Part Four, you will learn which behaviors people need to adopt to enable data and analytics in the project management practice that will ensure an evidence-driven model based on maximized knowledge.

Putting it all together

Part Five of the book merges the crucial factors of purpose, knowledge and behavior for the journey to data-informed practices. It provides an overview of how those elements can interact effectively to achieve the ultimate goal of improved delivery performance.

The interaction and proper balance between the three factors enable improved project delivery capabilities based on an enhanced focus on business value, ongoing strategic alignment between project delivery and business functions, and continuous improvement in terms of project delivery and innovation.

....

Lifting the capabilities

In a survey by NewVantage Partners, 92.2% of leading companies identified the cultural aspects as the biggest impediment to becoming a data-driven organization.[2] Research from McKinsey & Company shows that 70% of transformations fail due to a lack of engagement, accountability, appropriate collaboration, and suitable capabilities.[3]

It is clear that a successful transition to data-driven practices depends on the availability of data and the use of the right technology. It also relies on the right behaviors of people and a supportive culture that enables data and analytics. For the project management domain, there is, of course, no exception. Given the nature of project management and its history of slow innovation, it might be more critical than anywhere else.

In the following pages, you will learn the different elements we need to consider to make data and analytics work for the project management practice, unlock the hidden value of data and boost project performance and delivery.

Chapter takeaways

- Simply adding data and analytics into the mix can do more harm than good. Project management professionals need to enable those new capabilities, which requires a shift in people's behaviors and a general shift in attitudes and approaches.

- The key is the effective and balanced interaction between purpose, behavior and knowledge, with knowledge as your best tool for project delivery success.

- The success of a transition to data-driven practices depends on the availability of data, the use of the right technology, and the right behaviors of people.

PART TWO
Setting the Purpose

"Every person, organization, and even society reaches a point at which they owe it to themselves to hit refresh — to re-energize, renew, reframe, and rethink their purpose."

– Satya Nadella

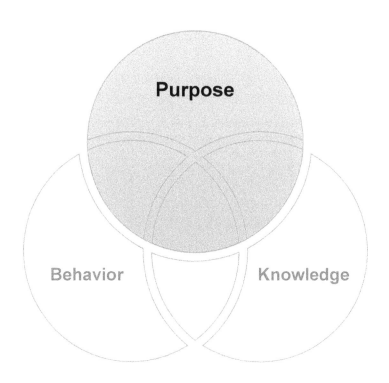

CHAPTER FOUR

Re-energize the Purpose of Project Delivery

The organizational purpose is the glue between an organization's mission or vision and the people. It serves to inspire and engage people to execute the company's mission.

However, according to Gallup, only thirty percent of employees in the US are engaged at work, and even the worldwide workforce is only thirteen percent engaged.[1] This is ultimately a call to action to ensure that employees understand and learn about the value of their daily work, which links to a sound and inspiring organizational purpose.

It is especially true for the project management practice. A project's purpose is usually about the value that a project and the resulting change would bring to the project client. When asking about a project's purpose, you are usually pointed to a business case that defines the parameters regarding the expected value from a change. But as Antonio Nieto-Rodriguez highlighted in an article for Harvard Business Review in 2021, a business case is not enough to claim that a project has a purpose.[2] Business cases are usually constructed based on logic, math and metrics; effectively, it's a numbers game that serves as a justification to undertake a project.

But purpose is also about the emotional side of things, which isn't measurable with numbers, metrics, or logical thinking. A purpose must highlight the importance of people's work and why they should care and engage. There are two questions we should be able to answer in a project management setting.

1. How valuable is my work to the organization and/or the project client?
2. What is in it for me?

Purpose statements should answer the Why question, i.e., justify why we are doing what we are doing. So the two questions above also could be extended into the following:

1. Why do we need this project?
2. Why am I doing this?

Both viewpoints need to be in sync to have full engagement from people. If a project and people's work are to provide significant value to a project customer, but the purpose doesn't match the project team's perception of invested effort versus outcome, then people will disengage. Invested effort is measured with emotional burden, learning, stress, progress and development. From the outside, a project may seem to provide good value based on money spent.

Engagement from people has a different formula.

People want more than knowing that their work is of value to someone. That doesn't necessarily mean getting paid more, a higher bonus, or a promotion. Of course, those are common motivators, but people also want to learn, progress and evolve. A career path in project management should provide the means to grow personally and professionally. People want to get better at what they do and improve how they manage and deliver projects. That means gaining experience and applying it to improve their practices.

The purpose of project management is two-fold. The purpose of the *project* links to what the project client receives in terms of value and the purpose of *project management practice* that is a discipline.

Given the challenges project teams face, with many struggling to get projects delivered on time and within budget, the question "Why am I doing this?" becomes increasingly difficult to answer. That means the true purpose of project management and delivery is lost over time, and project delivery teams often operate in a mode where upfront delays and major hiccups are already programmed. Also missing are growth, continuous improvement and evolution with business domains and project clients.

A survey conducted by PwC indicated that seventy-nine percent of business leaders believe an organization's purpose is central to business success.[3] According to a report from Harvard Business Review in collaboration with EY's Beacon Institute, eighty-four percent of surveyed executives said that purpose can affect an organization's ability to transform.[4] Hence, purpose is a key driver for change and is, therefore, a crucial enabler of transformation success.

But transformation should not be limited to transforming the project customer's business, otherwise the two Whys eventually will get out of sync.

In project management, we have that discrepancy in terms of project deliveries and the efforts that lead to those deliveries. It is time to rethink and redefine the purpose in the project management domain.

Microsoft CEO, Satya Nadella, wrote in his book *Hit Refresh.* "Every person, organization, and even society reaches a point at which they owe it to themselves to hit refresh—to reenergize, renew, reframe, and rethink their purpose."[5]

PART TWO

....

The importance of purpose

Purpose often gets linked to "doing good for the world and society" — usually referred to as higher purpose. I always struggled with such statements because it would mean that a company that is focused on profitability rather than contributing to society cannot be purposeful. The first thing that comes to mind when I think about contributing value and doing good are organizations like Greenpeace, United Nations, or Tesla (or any electric car manufacturer). The pandemic catapulted organizations like Pfizer or Roche into the top 20 of the 2022 Purpose Power Index.[6] Projects like improving sanitation and living conditions in developing countries are also perfect and admirable examples of purpose-driven initiatives.

But what about other companies? In a 2019 article for Harvard Business Review, Freek Vermeulen pointed out that companies in the management consulting, investment banking or tech sectors are more focused on profitability. In some cases, profit could be regarded as an organization's purpose.[7]

Naturally, many people have problems identifying with an organization's purpose if the company is actively engaged in environmental pollution or harming people's health. But the primary reason for an organizational purpose is for people to see that their work is meaningful and valuable to others, even if that doesn't fit the definition of social good.

Some years ago, I managed a digitalization project in a large international bank. My team delivered new digital capabilities to client account managers to make the whole process of onboarding a new bank customer faster, more efficient and less error-prone. The higher purpose was efficiency and competitive advantage, ultimately leading to more profit.

Simon Sinek said, "Profit isn't a purpose, it's a result. To have purpose means the things we do are of real value to others."[8] It means that profitability is an outcome while purpose is linked to the activities that produce the outcome. In the end, purpose gives meaning to project work.

Make it meaningful

Let's go further deeper into what purpose means in the project management domain, as this will be relevant to understanding its importance in employing data analytics in projects. I think many people struggle to point out the purpose of their respective projects.

A project's purpose should state why a project exists, giving some justification for its execution and its meaning. A purpose statement is very relevant because it should always be something to come back to, to remember why a project is being done. That ensures people are not going off track and following a direction that isn't aligned with the project's aims. A purpose should be like a guiding star people can identify with so that they engage and take ownership of their actions.

Robert E. Quinn and Anjan V. Thakor described a purpose-driven employee as one who takes ownership instead of minimizing their efforts. Someone who prioritizes common interest over conventional self-interest.[9] There must be a common understanding and an alignment regarding purpose within the project organization. Mark D. Steele, author of the book *Projects on Purpose 2.0*, argues that "each component of the project social system (...) has to share the same purpose or at least compatible purposes" to deliver successful projects.[10] A shared purpose should also include aspects of innovation and organizational design.

> *There's no point buying into a purpose that is unlikely to be achievable.*

In other words, a shared purpose also requires alignment in terms of the project organization and its maturity to support the realization of the common purpose. There's no point buying into a purpose that is unlikely to be achievable. Ignoring the executability of a project is a dealbreaker for fulfilling a project's purpose and almost always leads to failure. As highlighted by Quinn and Thakor, doing well under a higher purpose requires the ability to execute plans and, therefore, takes relevant capabilities and operational excellence.[9]

Ignoring the important factors of project management excellence and innovation eventually leads to a disconnect of people from purpose due to a lack of belief and faith in the authenticity of a stated vision.

Negativity spreads, with people becoming more reactive, switching eventually to a survival mode and focusing primarily on their interests.

A sound purpose should trigger optimism despite adversity and turbulence. It is meant to set free hidden energy, bind people together and foster an environment of trust, transparency and accountability.

Excellence, success and personal fulfillment are the consequences of purpose.

The importance of purpose alignment

An effective purpose that drives performance, needs to align with the project management practice and the overall purpose and strategy of the organization. Each layer builds on top of the other, as in figure 6.

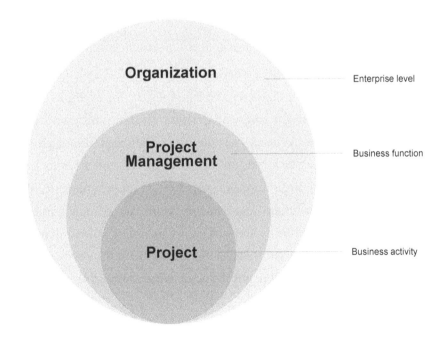

Figure 6: Purpose alignment

A misaligned structure would cause gaps in engagement and accountability, likely resulting in disconnects of people and teams, siloed and inconsistent practices, and a lack of knowledge sharing. Ultimately progress and evolution stall. Many project failures have their root cause in such misalignments.

Continuous alignment of the project delivery practice

It should now be evident that organizations evolve and progress to ensure their competitiveness in the market. The organization runs a business strategy that needs to be implemented and executed by the different business functions within that organization. As illustrated in figure 6, the discipline of project management is a distinct business function within an organization. It implements guidelines, frameworks and supporting methods to ensure that its activities (projects) can be executed effectively in alignment with overarching business strategies.

Effective business functions need to align with the organizational strategy regarding their maturity and capabilities. For example, some technology firms rely on frequent changes to their software tools, often deploying new versions multiple times each day. This might be a crucial part of the organization's business model and strategy, but change delivery functions and their capabilities must support it. The project management function has an important role here, as projects are usually carried out in all areas of an organization. A low maturity level of the project management practice could affect the performance of another business function and block an organization from reaching the best possible performance.

Antonio Nieto-Rodriguez highlights that the future of the organization is built on projects and the delivery of change.[11] Projects are essential for the organization's long-term success.

Given the importance of the discipline of project management, it is essential to maintain a thriving practice with the highest standards and most advanced methods to run and deliver projects. An irregular approach to reviewing project management practices with minor adjustments is no longer acceptable, primarily because of fast-changing conditions and environments.

Imagine an organization that worked as it did twenty or thirty years ago, using phones, postal mail and fax machines as its primary communication methods. It wouldn't survive in a world where messages travel the globe in seconds or less.

The purpose of project management must include value delivery. That means continuously improving the ways of operation and aligning them with the customer's needs and capabilities. Not using data and analytics for project delivery purposes is like ignoring the existence of smartphones. It won't eliminate your ability to communicate, but it will slow you down significantly. You have a handicap when it comes to being informed and communicating fast.

Projects are essential for the organization's long-term success.

Project management is of such importance that it simply cannot afford to run behind modern practices.

....

Project performance and value delivery

Projects aim to deliver the best value, which requires the best possible performance. The fundamental understanding is that value (and the *perception* of value) are relative to the starting point. A project should solve a problem (the starting situation) and lead to an intended outcome (the target situation). The outcome should achieve the target. The job of the project is to replace the starting situation with the target situation providing value to the project customer, as you can see in figure 7.

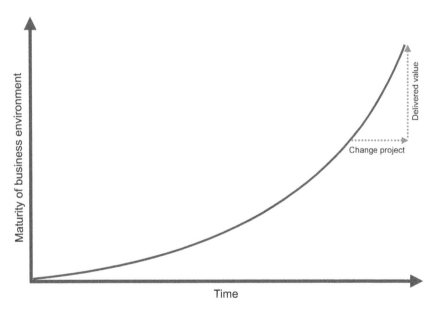

Figure 7: Value/time correlation

The delivered value raises the maturity of the respective environment to the project, which creates a new starting point for the next change project. What was considered value a few years back wouldn't be so today because the starting situation (the maturity level) has changed with evolution and growth. The maturity increased, with a likely impact on complexity. Think about how an organization evolves and becomes more mature with every change.

Let's take the German fashion retailer Zalando. Founded in Berlin in 2008, the company started as an online shoe retailer for the German market. It rapidly expanded its operations to other countries, launching new online retail sites, followed by the launch of subsidiaries for services such as payment processing and marketing activities for the group. All those changes required projects which contributed to the firm's growth and evolution. From a project management point of view, it needed to mature and become more structured while scaling efforts to the size of the company. Clearly, in terms of value delivery from projects, Zalando would have different measures and expectations today than it had ten years ago.

Generally, the growth of a firm inevitably results in the development and maturing of project management practices. This is usually seen in the form of project management training, setting up a project management office (PMO), establishing project management frameworks and applying an overall more structured approach to the delivery of projects.

The importance is in synchronizing efforts to evolve, grow and progress. To deliver value to the full extent expected of a demanding business, both the receiving business domain and the delivering project management domain need to be in sync in terms of their maturity levels. Otherwise, limited, or possibly no, value would be delivered.

A more illustrative formula would be:

$$\frac{\text{Maturity Level of Project Management}}{\text{Maturity Level of Business Domain}} \times \text{Change} = \text{Value}$$

As in a fast-growing company like Zalando, the maturity of all domains, including project management, needs to grow synchronously. With digital transformations, data-driven practices and emerging technology rapidly on the rise, increasing the capabilities and the maturity of various business areas, project management needs to ensure that it keeps pace in terms of capabilities and performance.

Chapter takeaways

- Purpose is about the emotional side of things. Therefore it must highlight the importance of people's work and answer why a project should be conducted and why they should care and engage.

- A sound purpose triggers optimism despite adversity and turbulence. It is meant to set free hidden energy, bind people together and foster an environment of trust, transparency and accountability.

- Purpose alignment ensures that the different business functions in an organization are synchronized in their efforts to evolve, grow and progress. They align in terms of maturity and capabilities and work effectively toward common strategic goals.

CHAPTER FIVE

(Re-)Enable Evolution

With the increasing importance of projects, the project management practice must continue to grow and evolve. As discussed, stalled progress results in a capability gap that causes misalignment, missed expectations, missed opportunities, and eventually results in a growing incidence of project failures.

Project management is an evolutionary practice based on learning from practice, so it relies heavily on knowledge, access and continuous growth. That means focusing efforts on optimizing available knowledge resources. For too long, project management was based only on knowledge silos and an overreliance on experience and human skill, although humans were not designed for accurate forecasting due to a general over-optimism.

It is, in a way, a paradox. Projects are all about forecasting and predicting events in the most precise and accurate way possible. But we keep ignoring the advances of science, knowing that we need those capabilities to address our natural shortfalls. It almost feels like having ignored the invention of automobiles, we keep using horse carriages for our day-to-day activities.

To deliver value to project customers, the project management practice must accept the delivery of value itself. That value is found in evolving practices and knowledge, and this means accepting the value and capabilities of data and analytics.

In this chapter, we will look at what it takes to re-enable the evolution of the project management practice and what such an evolution should look like.

....

Deliver learning, experience, knowledge and progress

Randy Bean, CEO of NewVantage Partners, used the expression "Fail fast, learn faster" to highlight how today's organizations are impacted by data and how data can be used to improve performance and efficiency, and gain competitive market advantage. Bean's key message is that failure is the foundation of innovation. Companies are forced to innovate due to an ongoing disruption and increasing pace of change.[1]

Projects are no longer constructed to deliver linear change. Instead, they have become vehicles for ideas, exploration and learning, with the expected outcome of growth and innovation.

Given that the path to innovation is plastered with failures, learnings, new experiences and new knowledge, this has never been more important. Accordingly, projects deliver more than just change to a business domain; they provide a learning experience that delivers new knowledge.

The challenge for project professionals and stakeholders is accepting this value proposition. Learning has always been part of project management practice, but today's turbulence, uncertainty and complexity require this aspect to be formalized further. No project is a waste. We always will have failures, but the biggest failure is not learning from them.

> *We always will have failures, but the biggest failure is not learning from them.*

Make learning a key project deliverable

As a project management activity, lessons learned are not always given the importance they deserve. Based on the evolutionary character of project management, they need to be seen as a benefit, not just as a key element of project management practices. Lessons learned become a measurable project deliverable, contributing to the outcome of a project.

Unfortunately, in many organizations, Lessons Learned sessions are only conducted as part of project protocol, to get something off people's chests and move on. Often, such sessions are not conducted at all because of time pressures to get going with the next project.[2] This is especially so when projects are deemed successful by the customer, as the expected scope was delivered. In those cases, no one is usually interested in conducting a Lessons Learned session.

But let the project fail, and the project sponsor and senior stakeholders demand a detailed post-mortem and analysis of lessons learned. This appears to be protocol because, of course, you cannot simply move on after a failed delivery. A project without delivered documentation or artifacts, including the documented outcomes and actions from a Lessons Learned session, can be practically considered a failure because the delivery is incomplete.

Address the flaws of 'Lessons Learned'

The Lessons Learned sessions too often turn into a blame game rather than a learning exercise.

Statements such as, "Of course, we couldn't develop the software as expected because there were issues with the design or architecture" may ring a bell. Nobody wants to admit a failure, so when confronted with such a possibility, people go into defense mode, behaving in a "Cover my ass" and "It wasn't my fault" way. That means true lessons are rarely learned.

Instead, these sessions need to be transformed into team-focused meetings that are measured and scored for lesson and learning outcomes.

We talked earlier about value delivery. As long as accurate, truthful and transparent lessons are produced as part of a project, there is value to be learned and made available for the wider project management audience to consider in any future project.

This part should never be skipped. It should be explicitly stated in the project charter as a mandatory deliverable.

Projects are not unique

Current teachings from leading project organizations such as the Project Management Institute (PMI) and Association for Project Management (APM) claim that a project is a unique endeavor with special and unique characteristics.[3, 4] The rationale is that each project produces a particular product or service as an output. Accordingly, the project requires tailored efforts and elements to achieve its goal.

Given how projects are currently handled, we could argue that projects are unique constructs — however, they should not be seen as unique pieces of work. Most work packages in a project are, at their core, clones of something already done before, often with minor variations.

PMI used to define projects in their Project Management Body of Knowledge (PMBOK) as temporary and unique. In more recent versions of the PMBOK, that statement has changed to something that accounts for repetitive tasks.

The PMI PMBOK Guide (2013) says, "Every project creates a unique product, service, or result.... Although repetitive elements may be present in some project deliverables and activities, this repetition does not change the fundamental, unique characteristics of the project work."[5]

However, an ongoing emphasis on the uniqueness of projects throws a shadow over another critical element at the core of projects and project management: that a project should always build on knowledge and experience from previous projects.

Continually promoting the unique nature of projects tells the responsible project manager to push the reset button for each project and start entirely from scratch. That means each project kicks off with an artificial handicap and the burden of being special and unique.

The Sisyphus effect

For projects and project managers, in particular, it means the current way of running projects has something of a Sisyphus effect. Sisyphus is a figure from ancient Greek mythology who was forced to repeatedly roll a rock to the top of a mountain, only to watch it roll down again.

If we map this myth onto projects, managers are doing something similar. They start every project almost from blank paper (the foot of the mountain), deliver a project (the top of the mountain), and then start over with the next project. If only projects learned properly from previous experience and similar project undertakings, they would not have to start over at the foot of the mountain with every single project.

Any project should be able to start closer to the top of the mountain.

Instead of starting from scratch all the time, any project should be able to start closer to the top of the mountain, with the result that the way to the top for any new project would be shorter and the risk of failure would be lower.

Learn about uncertainty

Improving project management practices and adopting new innovative ways of working effectively comes down to sharpening our ability to forecast and deal with uncertainty. Ideally, we would get to a state where we can accurately predict events, risks and any opportunities we can benefit from to deliver projects successfully.

But nobody can perfectly predict such events to provide a delivery guarantee. It is simply not possible with anything located in the future, even though our instinct is to crave certainty. People are usually uncomfortable with ambiguity and uncertainty. Humans prefer to be in control — it provides a feeling of order and achievement and makes us feel good.

With uncertainty, we are afraid we'll misunderstand or miss something. That is why we are so uncomfortable with uncertainty, complexity and ambiguity; it feels like we are not in control. So managing is about learning to deal with those feelings.[6] To become more comfortable with uncertainty, we need to engage with and embrace uncertainty instead of ignoring or fighting it.

Embracing uncertainty means getting another perspective which helps us be more open to experimentation and see opportunities rather than just risks. We need uncertainty for our aim to progress, as it provides clarity on what you can (and can't) control and what really is uncertain.

The future is inevitably uncertain, and improving the accuracy of our forecasts starts with getting another perspective on uncertainty that doesn't necessarily reduce it to something negative.

How uncertain are projects?

In the project management world, uncertainty is usually associated with the practice of managing project risks, as risks are defining events that may happen and impact the course of the project, either negatively or positively. However, many make the mistake of interchangeably using the terms risk and uncertainty, indicating that they mean the same thing. Risks are events that may or may not happen, so we are uncertain if risks are materializing.

To clarify the difference, let's first understand a bit better what uncertainty means.

The Cambridge Online Dictionary defines uncertainty as "a situation in which something is not known, or something that is not known or certain."[7] In his book *How to Measure Anything*, D.W. Hubbard describes uncertainty as "a state of limited knowledge where it is impossible to exactly describe the existing state, a future outcome, or more than one possible outcome."[8] This leads us naturally to the question of how we can possibly manage something we are uncertain about, and effectively do not know of. And which is therefore impossible to predict.

Given those distinctions, risks in projects are based on knowledge and experience regarding events that could happen. We can articulate such risks and quantify their probability and impact to a certain degree. On the other hand, uncertain events are outside of people's awareness, and we cannot articulate them or quantify their probability.

In 2002, United States secretary of defense, Donald Rumsfeld, made a statement that is often referred to in the context of projects and change as it helps clarify the concepts of uncertainty and risks. Rumsfeld said:

> *"Reports that say that something hasn't happened are always interesting to me because, as we know, there are known knowns; there are things we know we know. We also know there are known unknowns; that is to say, we know there are some things we do not know. But there are also unknown unknowns—the ones we don't know we don't know. And if one looks throughout the history of our country and other free countries, it is the latter category that tends to be the difficult one."[9]*

In a construction project, you may have a risk that weather conditions will change tomorrow. It is an unknown, but you are fully aware that it exists and could happen. On the other hand, uncertainty refers to events we cannot predict.

We'll look at the knowns and unknowns in more detail in Chapter Ten.

So if uncertainty is increasing, how can project managers handle such unforeseeable events? They are fishing in the dark and must expect to get hit by something they can't see or imagine coming. They cannot even prepare a mitigation plan as they would when managing project risks.

Imagine you are taking a trip in your car on the highway. As the driver, you are the project manager who needs to steer the vehicle until you arrive at your destination. Naturally, there are risks involved. Traffic jams or accidents could impact your journey and therefore need to be considered in your planning. Uncertainty could come in sudden changes in weather conditions or even highly catastrophic events such as earthquakes. This natural uncertainty is attached to anything that relates to future events. However, we usually have some confidence in our forecasts based on our ability to handle known risks with our experience, skills and knowledge.

But as uncertainty steadily increases, we, in turn, lose confidence. On a car journey, it could mean losing visibility; the street becomes foggy to the point where we are almost driving blind. Reduced capability increases uncertainty as we may be hit by something we haven't seen coming. How can we handle these situations? And how can project managers prepare for such unknowns and highly uncertain events in projects?

The answer is that they can't. The nature of uncertain events is that they come out of the blue and are rarely on anybody's radar.

The better question to ask is, "What if we convert uncertainty into certainty?" In their excellent book *Radical Uncertainty*, John Kay and Mervyn King differentiate between resolvable and radical uncertainty.[10] As the naming implies, resolvable uncertainty can be resolved. It is like a puzzle that has an answer. Find the solution and you have addressed and effectively removed the uncertainty. On the other hand, Kay and King refer to radical (or non-resolvable) uncertainty as mysteries that cannot be measured and, therefore, cannot be resolved with probabilistic means.

Examples of such radical uncertainty are often referred to as *Black Swans.* This term received a lot of attention in the project management domain, and is based on a theory developed by Nassim Nicholas Taleb in his book *The Black Swan.*[11] Black Swan events are very rare, highly unlikely and almost impossible to predict. Yet, when they do happen, they have a catastrophic impact. Black swans were and always will be present in projects and cannot be predicted.

Increasing uncertainty means an increase in resolvable uncertainty.

Increasing uncertainty means an increase in resolvable uncertainty and blurriness that can be addressed and managed. In the following chapters, we will see that this will not be possible with traditional methods. Increasingly, projects are hit by disruptive events that were not foreseen due to the limitations of traditional project management approaches.

Develop a vision for the practice

Kay and King make the important point that evolution would not happen without uncertainty. And project management is an evolutionary practice based on uncertainty, learning from practice, and therefore heavily relies on knowledge, access to knowledge, and continuous growth.

Therefore, re-enabling the evolutionary nature of project management practice requires a transformation. It requires change and people to drive this change. And this takes a vision that aligns with the purpose of project management. The vision will effectively draw the picture of what one wants to achieve to meet the purpose. In his book *The Vision Driven Leader*, Michael Hyatt highlights that a vision clarifies the future and prepares people for what is coming.[12]

With knowledge as a key driver for growth and evolution, investing in knowledge is vital. That requires changing the behaviors of project management practitioners, as knowledge needs to be maintained, nurtured, and to be most effective, it needs to be shared.

What is the point in accumulating knowledge if that knowledge is soon discarded?

And that is what is happening in many organizations. Project managers diligently put together schedules, budget calculations and forecasts, stakeholder maps, and risk registers, only to throw them in a random Sharepoint folder once the project is delivered. Effectively, this is a linear project economy, with knowledge built up and thrown away, as shown in figure 8.

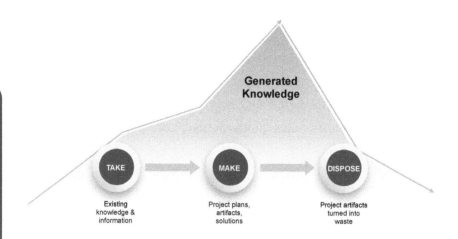

Figure 8: Linear project economy

This operating model blocks learning and evolution. The best we usually get out of projects is an addition to the experience of a project manager and a project team. The lessons learned go into tacit knowledge, rather than explicit knowledge that could be used for widespread learning and improvement.

Other organizations are a bit smarter by forcing project professionals to use online project management tools that ensure, for example, all project schedules or risk registers are held centrally in one place, using a common format.

Project data is valuable knowledge and is critical to make sense of past projects, identified patterns and resulting insights. We learn from them to improve future project delivery practices.

The circular project economy

In *Creating a Learning Society*, Joseph E. Stiglitz and Bruce C. Greenwald note that closing knowledge gaps is central to growth and development.[13]

In project management, a crucial part of this process is to stop throwing away valuable knowledge in the form of project artifacts. It's like when people behaved as if the earth had endless resources and thought that constantly producing piles of plastic waste was not harmful. They didn't realize that waste harms environmental health and holds a lot of value that could be reused.

Hence, the linear model needs to be replaced by the circular project economy model (figure 9) based on the steps Take — Improve — Make — Share. It follows the primary idea of continuously building and aggregating knowledge by recycling project artifacts and data.

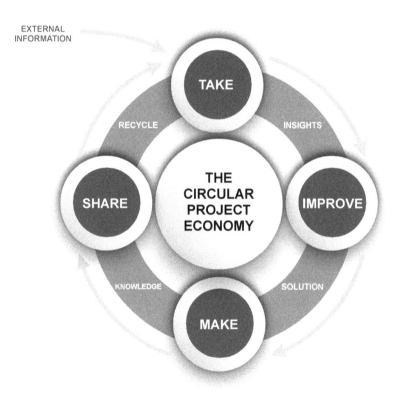

Figure 9: The circular project economy model

In short, we must take available knowledge, make sense of the combined knowledge to improve outcomes, create the solution and learn, and share the newly gained knowledge for injection into future projects.

Take

As with the linear approach, we start by taking our existing knowledge to initiate a project. The project team owns the experience, specific domain knowledge, and skills required to build and deliver a solution. It gathers information to elaborate on any risks or opportunities related to the project.

You may get additional information from external sources. A simple example could be a project management guide, any specific guidelines on Agile or SAFe (Scaled Agile Framework) practices, available documentation on the internet on best practices for a data migration project, or spreadsheet templates that could be useful for a project. No project manager knows everything, and, depending on the nature of the project, we usually rely on far more than experience and project management knowledge resources internal to an organization.

I once took on a project which required sourcing a software solution from an external provider. I needed to run an RFI (Request for Information) followed by an RFP (Request for Proposal). At that time, I had no experience with such processes and was looking for information on how best to run software sourcing projects. I needed to know what steps to include, best practices, templates, etc. There was limited information available internally at the organization, including certain rules and policies to follow. Elsewhere I found a few useful books with best practices for such projects, including some valuable resources and templates to use as a guide. In other words, I sought external information, selected the snippets that were relevant to my project, and mapped and tailored it according to the project requirements, applicable policies, and so on. I created knowledge from the collected information.

Improve

This step is about sense-making. You have selected all this knowledge concerning a project, and it is time to make sense of it. It is about building options for a solution to the project problem. The primary elements that play a role here are creativity, experimentation and collaboration. It is the stage where proofs-of-concept take place to determine the suitability of a potential solution.

Let's say we need to run a data migration project. We have a clear scope but not yet the right solution. If you've done such a project, you'll know it is often a complex beast with multiple pathways available. Depending on the complexity, there may be brainstorming workshops held first to make use of collective intelligence toward the elaboration of possible options for a solution.

And what is the improvement here? The input at this stage is the insights that derive from the combined knowledge from different available sources. Generating insights from combined knowledge (see the Make step) results in new knowledge. Remember that project management is an evolutionary construct, and each project conducted adds to the project manager's experience. Experience is knowledge, which increases with additional project experience. Combining this with others' grown knowledge generates collective insights that contribute value to a project.

By coming up with new creative options, experimenting, and working collaboratively, this stage contributes to new experiences and, eventually, additional knowledge. It's an improvement because people learn what works and what doesn't by experimenting with solution options and exchanging their knowledge.

Make

The Make stage is where the knowledge accumulated in the previous two steps is used to decide the implementation solution.

It is built on collected information and evidence such as proofs-of-concept or insights from peers who used similar solutions before in other projects and shared their experiences. Deciding which solution to implement is an informed process.

Implementing the decided solution creates new knowledge and adds to the experience. A projected way may need ongoing correction as previously unknown risks or issues appear, tasks may take longer than estimated, and the delivery date may be missed. It is effectively the stage where a significant portion of the learning process in a project takes place.

Share

This is the most important step of this model as we need to ensure that all the experience, learning, failures and success — in other words, the knowledge increment — get recycled for other future projects to use. This knowledge becomes part of the Take stage in a future project, along with any additional knowledge increments that accumulated over time. Shared knowledge is grown knowledge.[14]

Imagine you are conducting another data migration project of a similar kind, and you can access insights from twenty previous projects of a similar nature. Some may even be partially identical in terms of tasks, used technologies, etc. How useful would that be?

This will eventually make a significant difference. By injecting information from similar historical projects into the Take step, then running analytics to generate otherwise hidden insights to improve, we revive the evolutionary character of projects and lift the capabilities of project management practice to a new level of effectiveness.

While this looks and sounds easy, the injection of data, although produced by the same project professionals, could become a hurdle. It requires a change in thinking and, as mentioned before, data and analytics need to be enabled as a contributor to knowledge.

Engagement is the problem

While such a change in people's thinking and behaviors is a fundamental shift in the project management space, it doesn't mean the change itself must be hard, or that you should expect major resistance.

There's a common view that people don't want to change. That they are change-averse and prefer to play out their status quo bias of "It always worked this way, so why change?"

There are two arguments against this way of thinking.

First, the statement "It has always worked this way" is counterproductive as it implies that nothing ever needs to change. If true, that would be the end of projects. Projects exist to change things, and change exists to progress and evolve.

Second, most people are not change-averse. This is especially so for project professionals. After all, change is their daily business; they deliver it day in and day out. How can there be change resistance? Of course, there is a difference between delivering and experiencing change. Most people do not have a problem with change, however, they need to be made part of the strategy and the journey, as they work hands-on with projects every day. What often becomes a block is when the change is decided at upper management level, while the people affected are on the receiving end without any stake in the process.

Several years ago, I was on a consulting assignment in a large multinational organization. Project managers were told that the firm was to start rolling out agile practices and the CIO mandated that project teams must follow agile practices and methods.

Two things came to mind.

More than twenty years after the Agile Manifesto[15] was made public, this large international and otherwise advanced organization "suddenly" discovered agile practices. What took them so long?

As a project management practitioner, I appreciate agile methods but limiting my arsenal of delivery methods to them is a risk. It's like having a Swiss Army knife with only one tool, with all other options removed. It felt like sabotage, with no agility whatsoever.

My second point practically answered the first. The firm had tried at various times to roll out agile practices but badly missed getting buy-in from people. Of course, I wasn't the only one shaking my head when told that I was not allowed to use anything other than agile practices. Nobody got engaged in the mandated change; several teams

PART TWO

implemented something that looked like Agile but, in reality, had nothing to do with it. The transformation to Agile failed in the end.

The key to a successful transformation is less about the technicalities and more about people's engagement. Developing a sound vision and purpose that people can identify with helps empower people to take responsibility for implementing change.

Committing to purpose

If an organization wants to become agile, yet reduces the project delivery toolset by removing valid methodologies, it is not acting on the agile purpose. An organization interested in becoming data-driven does not have that purpose unless it changes to a data-driven or data-informed project management practice.

Many people link the purpose of project management to the delivery of value. The value of project management is "that it delivers consistent results, reduces the cost, increases efficiencies in the process, improves customer service and satisfaction, and provides a competitive advantage to your company."[16] And as PMI says, "Project management is the use of specific knowledge, skills, tools and techniques to deliver something of value to people."[17]

Judging by how project management in many organizations is not progressing in terms of knowledge and techniques, we could argue that project management's purpose is linked to delivering outputs but not necessarily to delivering value. Look at project management as a system that has its function and purpose. In her classic book, *Thinking in Systems*, Donella Meadows highlights that the way to deduce a system's purpose is by watching how the system behaves.[18]

> *A purpose must inspire project professionals.*

Purpose requires a commitment from everyone to follow through on goals. Hence a purpose must inspire project professionals to engage in the required change, take on accountability and produce the knowledge and collective intelligence to fulfill the purpose and project goals.

With the current hype around data, it is tempting to set a goal of being a data-driven organization. But the right behaviors need to be followed, at all levels, to re-enable the evolution of project management.

In the next chapter, we will look at what an evolving project management practice should look like.

Chapter takeaways

- Lessons learned are rarely given the required importance and often skipped because of time constraints. The fact that projects are not entirely unique makes it even more important that 'lessons learned' are considered a key project deliverable as they help to avoid constantly reinventing the wheel.

- Our natural instinct is to seek certainty and control. That makes us see uncertainty and ambiguity as enemies that need to be eliminated. Project teams and leaders need to develop a new perspective on uncertainty, which helps them lead more effectively and consciously by constantly being stretched for better performance.

- Re-enabling the evolution of project management requires people to be fully engaged and open to change. It takes a vision that shifts from a linear project economy to a circular model, building on the key elements of taking, improving, making, and sharing knowledge.

CHAPTER SIX

Deliver True Business Value

Projects deliver change that provides value. There is no point in undertaking a project if the outcome or deliverable is of no importance to the project customer. The customer invests money in a project just as you might invest in a haircut, arrange a birthday party, or even simpler things such as taking a cab or baking a cake. In the end, you expect something in return for money spent — something that changes things for the better. We usually evaluate our investments in terms of return on investment (ROI), which applies to any type of project. There should always be tangible, valuable results for a project customer. Benefits make a project worthwhile.

....

The value proposition of projects

The trigger for any project is the need for change. Projects are vehicles to deliver change most effectively and efficiently. The discipline of project management is in using knowledge, skills, tools and techniques to ensure that value is delivered as expected by the project customer. As PMI defines, "projects are a temporary effort to create value through a unique product, service or result."[1]

Projects are all about events expected to happen in the future, so there is naturally an element of uncertainty. Project managers need to combine their skills, experience and knowledge, and make the right decisions to define, manage and execute a plan. That plan will likely achieve defined targets in terms of required cost, effort, time, dependencies, as well as any risks or issues that may impact the planned project goals. Given the inevitable confrontation with uncertainty, project management relies heavily on knowledge and experience, not just skills and techniques.

Stakeholders expect value to be delivered through proven project management practices, and accumulated and tested project management knowledge.

Delivering projects vs. value

A project manager in a large international bank climbed the ranks and was keen to make it to director level. When he got onto a candidate list, his boss told him that to be promoted, he would need to meet his defined goals for that year — primarily one specific goal to implement and deliver a particular software in the business area he worked in. The message was clear: deliver the project as per the defined target, and he'd be promoted. "Per defined target" meant delivery on time, on budget and within a defined scope.

The project manager told me that the project was experiencing a lot of challenges, which put the delivery date (and therefore his promotion) at risk. Several issues with the quality of the software implementation required some rework and potentially a different direction to provide a stable solution. But that would take more time and result in higher costs. To avoid jeopardizing his promotion, the project was delivered on time and within budget and the defined scope. But the implemented software was patched together with band-aids to pass quality assurance tests and make it seemingly fit for production deployment.

It was a ticking time bomb, with a long list of pending items to follow up on, but what appeared to count most was achieved. The project manager kept his promise and delivered and was promoted up the ranks, only to move to another department a few months later, leaving behind a mess to clean up.

Was value delivered? Perhaps yes, because business users were able to start using new software which was supposed to improve their day-to-day business operations. But maybe not, because they were likely to run into issues with that software because of a fragile system. Is the project manager to blame for this scenario? Not necessarily, as long as he was transparent about the implications of the decision approach.

But in many project organizations, the primary goal appears to be to get a project across the finish line and tick the completion checkbox to claim victory and maintain a good track record of delivering projects. The root cause of this is often located in the organizational culture and underlying processes, specifically annual performance reviews and ratings based on the evaluation of performance goals. In addition, organizational politics and/or personal interests often take precedence over delivering true business value.

There's also the issue that nobody wants to see invested effort wasted. This could kick in when a project is delayed, resulting in firefighting scenarios and maybe weekend work when people are stretched to deliver the project. People want to see all this extra effort pay off, and

PART TWO

the more effort they invest, the more reluctant they are to terminate a project, even if that is the better option.

It's the effect of a common bias called sunk cost fallacy.[2]

With plenty of effort invested, they want to collect the reward simply by getting it done — even if the project doesn't deliver the intended business value. Instead of revalidating the value proposition, they just want to get it across the finish line. Delivery? Check.

But the primary focus of value delivery is often forgotten. And when projects deliver only for the sake of delivering, without providing value, then it feels like a tourist who makes an effort to travel somewhere, just to say "I have seen it" without actually having explored that location, its culture or the people. Wasted effort happens when projects don't deliver real business value.

Value beyond the business deliverable

Yet value is not the only business benefit achieved. It's possible to deliver valuable customer benefits but not meet cost and/or schedule targets. Consider popular sporting events like the FIFA Football World Cup or the Olympic Games. Nobody would deny that those events (at least most of the time) achieved their intended value. But the Olympic Games projects never deliver on their cost targets.[3] The FIFA World Cup in Brazil in 2014 was deemed a huge success, but economically, it was a failure.[4, 5]

Projects are often labeled a success because of the perceived value of delivered benefits. But meeting the benefits and scope goal does not make a project automatically successful. A project has to meet all the defined targets, including cost and schedule targets. The project value is often just limited to the scope of the project deliverables and if they generated the expected benefits. But value should be measured by reviewing the relationship between cost, schedule, and delivered benefits.

If a project overruns its budget, this usually decreases the perception of value, as it conflicts with the business case.

Missed delivery is not the only criteria for project failure

Project outcomes must be judged rigorously. That would mean the related project could still be considered a failure, even if a business deliverable was deemed successful because of its value.

In the end, timelines, target delivery dates, and budgets have meaning and aren't set just for fun. Of course, nothing can be guaranteed, but targets must be managed, and the project management organization must provide the project manager with all the tools to manage those

Labeling a project as a success despite schedule or budget overruns means accepting slippages.

targets as accurately as possible. Labeling a project as a success despite schedule or budget overruns means accepting slippages. The message should be, "Hey, we have missed those targets, so we need to investigate why that happened and how we can do better next time."

The purpose and mission of a project management practice should be to deliver value to project customers, continuously improve processes and ensure value is delivered.

This requires constant enhanced scrutiny of challenges. We do this by reviewing genuine project failures (did not deliver) and the reasons behind partial fulfillment (delivered only partially) or nearly missed project delivery (delivered, but the project did not go according to plan and almost failed). If projects frequently run at the edge and deliver only partially, then stakeholders lose trust and confidence. Figure 10 illustrates this.

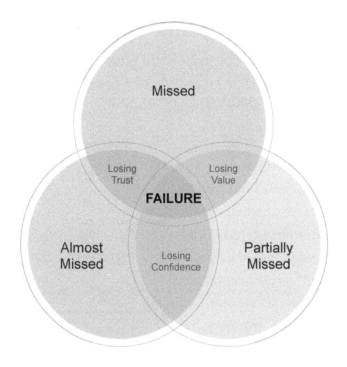

Figure 10: Treating near and partial misses like failures

A project management practice should not operate like an airline that labels a flight as fully successful just because the plane did not crash.

I was once on vacation flying from Mexico City to Cancun, and during the flight, there was oil spilling onto my seat. My first thought was, "If I ever get out of here alive, I'll never fly with this airline again." We don't want project stakeholders to think this way about our projects. In the end, the capabilities of delivering on project targets are driven by stakeholder trust and the awareness and confidence of the project team. Both require constant attention and nurturing.

> *If you frequently run projects with near misses, the risk increases that this will always happen.*

If you frequently run projects with near misses, the risk increases that this will always happen. It becomes normal. With project teams more often entering turbulence and stress, their focus increases on output but decreases on value outcomes.[6] The project team needs to verify what caused the near failure to ensure that the situation will not happen again. Treating near misses like failures, with the required post-mortems and lessons learned, not only establishes an understanding of what went wrong and improves robustness, but it also increases confidence and ultimately trust from stakeholders.

....

The value proposition of data-informed projects

The next question is what a data-informed practice can offer project management. What is the value proposition for using data and analytics in projects? How can it help us to get better at delivering projects?

Data analytics is a method of using data to guide decision-making.[7] We can differentiate between two distinct scenarios or questions that analytics can use to produce insights for better and informed decisions: deductive and inductive analysis.

Deductive analysis

Deductive analysis is based on a hypothesis and seeks to answer why something happened. For example, we may want to understand why projects in one particular area of an organization frequently have cost overruns. Analytics can identify patterns in data from past projects that could identify the root cause of overruns. Reasons could include discrepancies in estimation methods or the wrong use and allocation of resources (e.g., third-party contractors vs. internal staff). Analytics could confirm or disprove these hypotheses.

Inductive analysis

This type of analysis aims to predict what will likely happen based on historical information. A project manager may want to learn about third-party suppliers that will deliver on time and within certain cost constraints. Analysis of past projects and the different factors of the type of supplier, supplier profiles and delivery history, their reputation, delivery quality, the nature of delivery, estimates and complexity, provide insights that could help make appropriate decisions regarding the selection of the supplier, the timelines and risk mitigation plans.

With inductive analysis, we start with the objective for a particular project or problem and let analytics identify the relevant patterns around that objective.[8]

Analytics as a sparring partner

Analytics can turn data into information and knowledge by extracting patterns that help project teams make informed decisions. By adding data and analytics into the knowledge mix, there is less reliance on guesswork, intuition and gut feeling. It contributes to evidence-based decision-making.

Data and analytics and the deductive and inductive analysis approaches offer clear advantages for project teams.

At the same time, analytics serve as a sparring partner to project professionals, challenging their often preconceived opinions and ideas. Over time, people's assessments based purely on experience and intuition will improve by constantly being tested and exposed to data-driven insights. This is especially important because project decisions cannot always be made using data. There will remain many situations when project managers need to make quick decisions with no time for data analysis. While analytics help to improve the decision-making quality overall, it is not only based on the provisioning of insights derived from data but also on its role as a stressor to conventional human knowledge and judgment. It shapes and forms people's experiences and intuition.

Apply data-driven design thinking

With this in mind, there could be a risk of losing sight of the overall purpose of a change. The focus could be too much on data and becoming too analytical. The quantitative and qualitative views of a project problem need to be properly balanced and applied. Data and analytics can help generate the necessary insights to guide us towards solution finding. However, they are insufficient for an informed decision as they lack human input and tacit knowledge, something you won't find in a requirements document.

Think of an online shop like Amazon and its workflows and design. Analytics can provide insights into where to place a buy button to achieve the best customer conversion rates. But this is useless if the button isn't used because it's too difficult for the targeted user group to find.

This is where design thinking can be useful, as it is a human-centered technique that helps to maintain a focus on business needs and specific user requirements and, thus, on the purpose.

It is a method that supports the generation of qualitative and human-driven insights. This is especially useful when employing data-informed practices in projects, as we need to dance with data by asking questions, analyzing information, and challenging its validity. Design thinking is an iterative activity of exploring, experimenting, proving and disproving a hypothesis. Generating an insightful quantitative view requires interaction with qualitative views. That combination eventually creates high-quality solutions or decisions that fully align with a project's purpose. The qualitative perspective is based on user interviews, which help us fully understand their problems and pain points, and develop a hypothesis. The quantitative nature of data challenges that idea.

Some call this a data-driven design thinking process as it combines the concepts of analytics and design thinking. While it helps to reduce the risk of bias from the human qualitative input, it remains human-centric and user-focused.[9] Effectively, it ensures the right balance between different views and related insights.

The economic value of analytics

There is economic value in making the transition to data-informed projects. We want to clearly measure and understand the metrics behind the projected improvement, in this case, by introducing the capabilities of analytics towards a data-informed project delivery practice.

But it is difficult to put a dollar amount on the value of analytics.[10] To do so, we must fully understand what it should solve.

Analytics can reduce costs by spotting redundancies in project management processes, helping to reduce overall effort and the risks of frequent firefighting. It can help us better understand why certain things happened in past projects, e.g., frequent cost overruns for a particular type of project.

Wayne Eckerson is a thought leader in the business intelligence and analytics space. In his book *Secrets of Analytical Leaders,* he noted that the value of analytics generally increases as the focus shifts from past to present to future.[11] In other words, shifting the project management practice towards a higher emphasis on proactivity (vs. reactivity) and prediction (vs. reporting and monitoring) will unleash the full value of data analytics in projects.

The value comes from using optimized and properly orchestrated project management knowledge to make sense of the past and the present towards predictions for the future. Data and analytics can provide insights based on the past, and human experience, expertise and intuition can use them to project and evaluate scenarios.

As Eckerson argues, analytics help organizations make better and smarter decisions and move them to a more proactive model to foresee and address issues and opportunities before they occur. Given today's fast pace of change, this capability is essential to remain competitive.

Remove waste with lean management

The concept of lean management originated in an initiative by Toyota to optimize its car manufacturing and product development processes. They held one fundamental principle — to eliminate waste in the process, i.e., remove anything that doesn't add value to the end product.

Lean principles were adopted to make software development cheaper, faster and better through improvement measures such as unnecessary waiting times. Waiting times in software development processes are considered the biggest waste as they cause delays for the project and its delivery.

One important element of lean management is learning to identify which parts of a project produce waste, what is actual waste, and what is absolutely necessary.

In their book *Lean Software Development*, Mary and Tom Poppendieck suggested using value stream mapping to discover waste in the process.[12] The exercise involves drawing up all the steps in a process, from initiation to completion, including durations, to get a holistic view of the process. Value stream mapping helps find bottlenecks and wasteful activities. Figure 11 shows an example of this process.

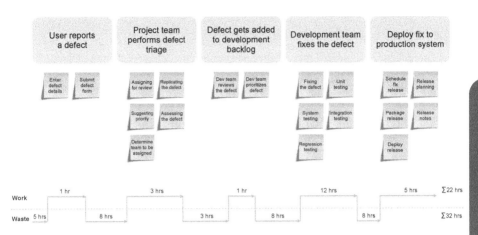

Figure 11: Example of value stream mapping

Lean management concepts apply to a process with a start and an end, just like a software development process or project.

In Chapter Five, I discussed the need for a circular project economy, which is a never-ending cycle. It is based on the concept of continuous improvement, one of the core principles of lean management. The key part is that each project and cycle bring small changes or increments of knowledge and intelligence in the form of new learnings and insights.

Turn waste into learning and knowledge

The primary goal of lean management is to identify and remove waste, but another goal should be to identify the incorrect labeling of something as waste. Using an exercise such as Value Stream Mapping in combination with the circular process economy model and process makes it apparent that project artifacts and knowledge are often (though not always deliberately) treated like waste and discarded.

Remember, though, that project management is evolutionary. At its core, it relies on knowledge building and learning, which must be considered when examining project management practices for true waste and waste that shouldn't be wasted.

....

Prepare for the future

It sounds obvious. Aren't projects all about preparing for future events?

Yet I would argue that most of what we do is making assumptions based on people's biased knowledge, lining up resulting tasks in a schedule, and bolstering the timeline with a contingency reserve that follows some questionable mental model. Of course, I am exaggerating somewhat, but I believe project teams are rarely prepared for the future, especially not for one that we expect to include turbulence and disruption as the new normal.

Oxford University uses the acronym TUNA (turbulence, uncertainty, novelty, ambiguity) in scenario planning to make it clear that today's environments are changing faster than ever, making projects highly unpredictable.[13] It's along the lines of the popular VUCA (volatility, uncertainty, complexity, ambiguity) acronym. Both make the same point, and, in terms of project management, it comes down to one important message: we have to find the means to be better prepared for the future.

Merely adding (and even increasing) a contingency reserve because of perceived uncertainty has nothing to do with being prepared.

Preparing for the future means improving the capability and culture of a project organization and its teams to be better prepared for unforeseen events and surprises that either could threaten the success of a project or represent an opportunity to take advantage of.

That requires the identification of trends and patterns to adopt an anticipatory way of operating in projects. Daniel Burrus writes in *The Anticipatory Organization* about hard and soft trends that we need to grasp to prepare for possible futures.[14] There are easy ways to identify hard trends (e.g., electric cars will become the norm). A soft trend is a possible future based on hard assumptions (derived insights from data) and soft assumptions (opinions, intuition).

It is important to continuously revalidate assumptions and watch for new emerging trends, as changes and disruptions are happening far more often.

Build anticipative capabilities

Strategic foresight techniques are usually applied to explore and validate future scenarios for strategic planning exercises in organizations. They are slowly making their way into the project management practice. One example is the Three Horizons method which can be used to discover early signs of potential change in environments.[15] It enables the identification of trends by combining viewpoints to examine the status quo (managerial mindset), what is likely to happen in the short- or near-term future (entrepreneurial mindset), and what is likely to materialize in the future (visionary mindset).[16] It helps people think about current assumptions and emerging trends to determine possible futures.

PART TWO

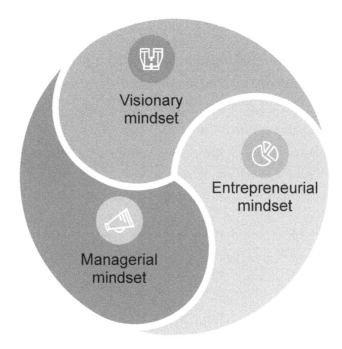

Figure 12: Three mindsets for horizon scanning

This does not predict the future but explores potential scenarios to better prepare and minimize the risk of project failure.

Managerial mindset

This mindset is about the status quo and the current paradigm. What do you know exists and works in a particular way? It reflects how things operate today. People don't want to change and do (at best) only minor incremental changes that will not alter Business-as-Usual (BAU). The managerial mindset serves as an assessment of today to prepare for possible future scenarios.

Entrepreneurial mindset

This mindset is about the near or short term, and is a bridge to the more distant future (visionary mindset). What is likely to change based on what we know of today's reality? Conflicts may arise when we connect this to the long-term vision, as it is a transition between now and a distant future that is highly uncertain.

Innovation and creativity are at their peak here, with increasing opportunities and risks.

Visionary mindset

This mindset is about the distant future and long-term vision for the project management domain. What is emerging and will be commonplace in the future? Looking at today's reality (status quo), which elements are trending to evolve (e.g., electric cars today, flying cars in the future)?

It is about making sense of social, economic and technical trends that are unlikely to realize today or in the near term and envisioning how those trends could become a reality in the distant future.

The greater the variety of the developed scenarios for possible futures, the better prepared teams will be for the commotion of change and disruption. Effectively, the project team increases the range of its response repertoire. Sharing those responses could also help other project teams prepare for future challenges.

Obsess with continuous improvement

With this increasing pace of change, rapid digitalization in organizations, and constantly changing messages, it is clear that project professionals cannot stand still. You will be left behind if you do not ride this evolution wave.

> *Today's reality is short-term projects with high agility.*

The project management space is full of inefficiencies, largely because of hesitation to embrace new ways of working and adopt a culture that drives continuous improvement through constant observation, experimentation, a higher appetite for risk, and openness to failure. The times when projects were designed in a linear, toll-gated and predictable way are over.

Project cycles have shortened because nobody can accurately plan for the years ahead. Today's reality is short-term projects with multiple iterations with high agility and constant exploration and discovery of new trends, threats, or opportunities.

The mandate is clear. Project managers cannot be just managers anymore. They must step up and lead by actively contributing to improvement measures and exercising agility and adaptability.[17]

The evolutionary mindset

Evolution does not happen by itself. It means continuous and ongoing change that must be initiated, enabled and followed through without stopping. While most people fully agree that project management is an evolutionary process, few contribute to it. An evolutionary mindset is required to actively drive things further.

So, what is an evolutionary mindset?

It goes beyond a growth mindset which uses failure as a source to learn and advance. An evolutionary mindset takes learning and uses it to improve and evolve project delivery processes and ways of working. Adopting an evolutionary mindset means including ourselves in the process. That means we learn about ourselves and our behaviors, how they contributed to a situation, and what we can learn from it. People are not exempt from change and evolution in the project management domain.

This is especially so in a new setup where knowledge is composed of data and analytics, experience and intuition. We must develop a holistic and integrative view of all players and contributors and the required changes to evolve.

Chapter takeaways

- Many project teams are operating under frequent turbulence and stress, risking missing crucial delivery deadlines. Such near misses need to be treated like failures as there is a risk of this becoming a constant state, leading to loss of trust and confidence of stakeholders and eventual inability to deliver.

- Applying data-driven design thinking helps to maintain the right balance between data and analytics and the more human-centric view from users. It ensures continuous focus on the business problem and project purpose.

- Project leaders and teams need to build more anticipative capabilities by employing modern techniques such as strategic foresight and horizon scanning. Adopting a combination of managerial, entrepreneurial and visionary mindsets helps us better grasp possible futures and scenarios based on current assessments and identified trends.

PART THREE
Knowledge: The Most Valuable Asset

"Knowledge has become the key economic resource and the dominant, and perhaps even the only, source of competitive advantage."

— Peter Drucker

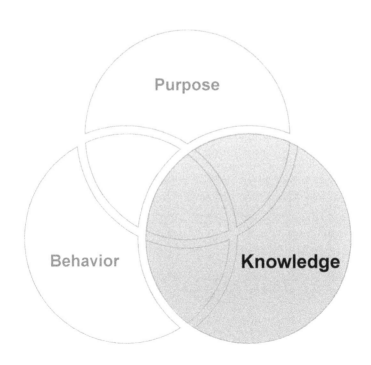

CHAPTER SEVEN

Understanding Project Management Knowledge

PART THREE

Knowledge is a crucial factor in the success of projects. A primary reason for ongoing high project failure rates is the lack of adequate knowledge transfer from past to future projects.[1] Improving knowledge management (KM) practices will significantly impact success rates.

This is especially so in an evolutionary and future-focused discipline like project management that relies on learning from experience. Knowledge is a crucial asset that requires appropriate management and constant exploration.

First, we must understand what knowledge means. In the context of this book, we differentiate between data, information and knowledge.

Data are symbols or signals that are captured and recorded (e.g., numbers or images).[2]

Information is data that is intelligible to the recipient or consumer.

Knowledge is the "cumulative stock of information and skills derived from the use of information."[3] It is information that is given context by being processed by the consumer. Knowledge earns meaning and value when actioned through decision-making. Actions based on acquired knowledge create value for project stakeholders.

> *Given the considerable economic value of knowledge, organizations must be able to continually build and acquire it.*

Given the considerable economic value of knowledge, organizations must be able to continually build and acquire it. And that requires appropriate knowledge management.

Knowledge management is the orchestration of knowledge. It includes people sharing tacit knowledge and the collection and organization of explicit content.[4] Knowledge management practices also require us to identify knowledge gaps before we can take measures to address them. Alan Burton-Jones, a senior lecturer at Griffith University in Australia, highlighted this need in 2003, including the difficulty of identifying tacit knowledge.[5] His explanation is shown in figure 13.

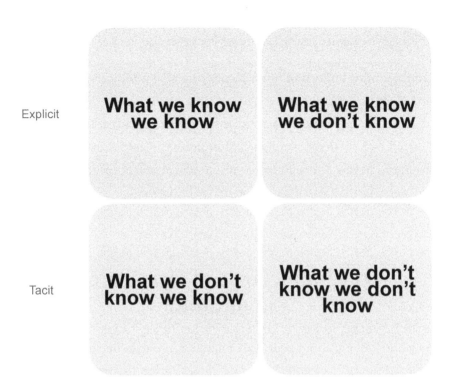

Explicit

Tacit

Figure 13: Identifying knowledge assets and gaps (Used with permission)[6]

Consider this model in the context of project management.

Explicit knowledge involves tangible, documented and stored knowledge assets such as project artifacts. These include project plans, schedules and technical documentation, produced and built from collected data and information. Project professionals put things into context and connect the dots to generate knowledge capital that can be easily shared.

"What we know we don't know" includes elements like unforeseeable risks or issues or a Black Swan event that have a significant impact.

Uncertainty exists in projects, and while we cannot grasp radical and unforeseeable uncertainty, it must be measured.

Organizations understand that identifying assets and gaps for explicit knowledge is relatively straightforward. Tacit knowledge is linked mainly to people's experience and intuition skills, and makes up a large portion of knowledge capital. It is difficult to capture and optimize, primarily because it requires a culture and mindset in which people are more open to sharing their (hidden) knowledge.

....

The importance of experience and intuition

As we talk freely about data, data analytics and data-driven practices, we might readily assume that data should drive the future and that people should adhere to data-derived facts and insights. Humans hold biases, so we can think of data analytics as a control function that spots when biased or irrational thinking kicks in and questions its logic and suitability.

Data and analytics cannot answer every question.

But data and analytics cannot answer every question. There's a danger that we get drawn into data and analytics and see them as the sole source of truth.

Data can never be so because it does not contain all the knowledge accumulated from experience, lessons learned and decisions made. Effectively, project management knowledge is based on people's experience, intuition and even gut feelings. That combination results in intelligence that project managers apply to steer their projects to successful outcomes. After all, projects are knowledge-driven.

Knowledge is also formed by the information we are exposed to and deem important. Using data and analytics effectively says existing knowledge and resulting intelligence are insufficient to make project decisions with high confidence of accuracy and precision. It doesn't mean experience and intuition are not required, as they are essential for truly informed decisions.

Don't get into the trap of banking everything on data and analytics because there are limitations. Only the combined intelligence from human experience, intuition, and data and analytics can achieve the best possible decisions. Intuition, experience and data all have their strengths and weaknesses, but in combination, they complement each other to build a powerful knowledge construct.

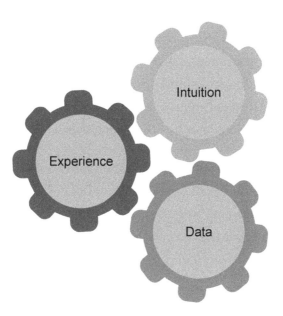

Figure 14: Experience, intuition and data form knowledge

Experience and intuition are essential contributors, and a data-informed project management practice won't work without them.

Experience

The Collins Online Dictionary defines experience as "knowledge or skill in a particular job or activity, which you have gained because you have done that job or activity for a long time."[7] The human experience differs from data because it is based on imperfect and inconsistent emotions. For instance, we remember what we experience, but usually forget certain parts after a while, making memories more abstract. This generates a unique type of intelligence.

In his book *Gut Feelings,* German psychologist Gerd Gigerenzer argues that if we couldn't forget, we would be completely overwhelmed by the amount of detail and information stored in our memories, which would slow the retrieval of relevant moments and experiences.[8]

Forgetting allows us to be objective and learn, which is especially important for project managers who deal with a high degree of uncertainty. Without cognitive limitations (including forgetting), which protect us from some of the dangers of possessing too much information, we would not function as intelligently as we do.

The data that project professionals produce mirrors their experience. It is a product of gained knowledge and expertise and captures practices, successes, failures and insights. While produced data involves hard facts, our experience puts data into context and interprets it so we can learn from it.

Intuition

Intuition is often referred to as instinct, a feeling in the gut, or a hunch, primarily because it is free of analytic reasoning and logic. When deciding intuitively, we "just know" about right or wrong and decide without the need for evidence or reason. But intuition is formed over time based on various factors that build intelligence. These include:

1. Data and information – we are exposed to information and knowledge that unconsciously drive views and behaviors. Our response depends on the type, insightfulness, importance and impact of the information.

2. Experience – scenarios that we experience can impact future decisions. Everything around us has an impact on our intuition.

3. Personality – personality types perceive the world and process information differently based on their experience.

PART THREE

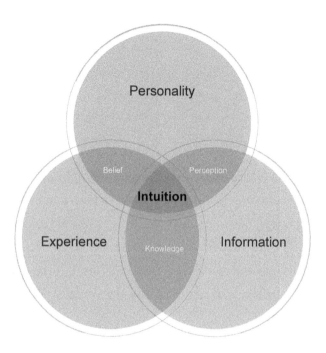

Figure 15: Components of intuition

So, we perceive the world by recognizing signs, gaining information from scenarios and environments, then processing the information using prior knowledge. This censoring and information processing mechanism contributes to our intelligence.

It is like our instinctive need to cry in certain situations. We do so because we are exposed to data and information that we perceive is linked to our personality and beliefs. It triggers an emotional effect that we express through tears. We usually can't control the response, and the trigger is not based on logical reasoning. But it tells us something that goes beyond a mere hunch and has a stake in decision-making.[9,10]

Intuition is based on what your subconscious has seen in the past

Experience forms intuition as it builds our opinions and views of right or wrong, and good or bad.

When project management teams fail to deliver or have a streak of failures, people become hesitant and cautious, impacting actions and decisions. They start to believe that they will likely fail again.

Even if the data and information indicate success, and you're normally optimistic and embrace risk, belief is usually stronger than perception. Experience and resulting beliefs have a strong impact. For instance, let's say a project manager has many years of experience leading a particular type of project to successful outcomes. They develop a strong conviction about their capability to succeed in a similar future project. Data and information may indicate a different view (e.g., based on organizational structures and constraints, cultural barriers, politics, etc.). The project manager may perceive this as a challenge but not a barrier, leading to a more intuitive judgment regarding their role and engagement in that project.

The impact of intuition

Intuition and gut feeling should not be seen as primary factors in decision-making. However, intuition is formed over time and holds valuable input that complements the insights derived from data and analytics.

Swiss psychiatrist Carl Jung wrote that "intuition transmits perception in an unconscious way" which has the potential to generate ideas, images, new possibilities and ways out of seemingly hopeless situations.[11]

....

Data and analytics in the knowledge mix

With the increasing importance of data and analytics, organizations have moved from dealing with data as an isolated construct or tool to something to be integrated into an organization's knowledge. The ability of data and analytics to generate insights to reduce uncertainty will make decisions and projects more informed. It fills a natural knowledge gap that grows exponentially if not taken care of.

Enabling data and analytics to contribute to our overall knowledge requires interaction with existing human knowledge. It needs knowledge about data to determine what is relevant and should be collected. It needs knowledge of the project and applicable business domains to guide analytics as a technique to identify patterns and generate insights. The insights derived from data and analytics interact with experience, domain expertise, and intuition to lead to action, as shown in figure 16.

PART THREE

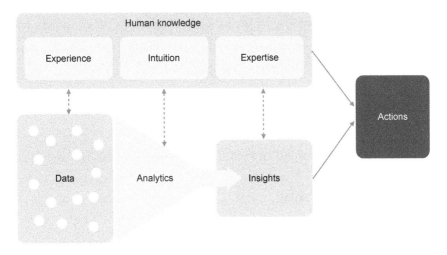

Figure 16: Interaction of human knowledge and data and analytics

To make this more tangible, let's look at an example.

To plan a project for the implementation of an ERP (Enterprise Resource Planning) system, we want to build the work breakdown structure (WBS), the project schedule, and a risk register. To achieve this, we collect project management data from similar past projects to gain insights that help with the planning process. Project managers who are specialized in ERP projects know the criteria to filter out the necessary project management data. Further project-specific criteria could be derived from the business case or other information, such as industry, stakeholder complexity, ERP vendors and modules, IT infrastructure constraints and customization requests. Collecting this data allows human knowledge to apply the right analytics techniques based on the type of data we are looking for. The focus is on schedule data, possibly on different phases or tasks of the project and their typical durations, what risks we need to observe in the schedule, and so forth.

Additional human experience and expertise insights could relate to the available resources, skill levels and motivations. That means we may adjust a project estimate based on analyzed data from similar past projects, depending on the input from tacit human knowledge.

Eventually, combining those insights leads to action in the form of a decision about a project schedule, captured risks, etc. Following through on this action and executing the decision adds experience.

Insights vs. learning

An insight differs from learning in many ways. As the word suggests, insight is about having an inside view of something. We do in-depth analysis to inspect what is going on for a particular type of project.[12]

According to Cambridge Dictionary, insight is "the ability to have a clear, deep, and sometimes sudden understanding of a complicated problem or situation."[13] Imagine insight as a bulb that lights up a room – you suddenly become aware of things you couldn't have seen without it. How we use that insight is a different story.

Analytics and big data certainly have their place in project management, as long as those new contributors interact with existing human knowledge to complement insights and eventual sense-making.

The hype around data and analytics makes it tempting to forget those aspects and believe they will magically provide insights for our most complex decisions. But data and analytics alone do not help at all. They sit idle at the front door of project management knowledge. Human experience, expertise and intuition need to take the initiative and open the door, so analytics and big data can participate in the knowledge party.

This requires a closer look at data, particularly in the project management domain. We'll cover this in the next chapter.

Chapter takeaways

- People risk being drawn in and seeing data and analytics as a single source of truth. But experience, intuition and gut feelings are also essential contributors to project management knowledge.
- Intuition is often ridiculed as a mere hunch, but it is an important part of our intelligence. It forms over time based on experience and information, holding valuable input that complements the insights derived from data and analytics.
- Enabling data and analytics to contribute to the overall knowledge requires interaction with the existing human knowledge. This leads to genuine insights and action, generating valuable new experiences.

PART THREE

CHAPTER EIGHT

Addressing the Knowledge Gaps

Before leveraging project data and analytics to improve project management performance, we must identify the exact knowledge gaps. These can vary between organizations, but the root causes are usually the same. Our task is to understand what drives the creation of those gaps, uncover hidden knowledge areas, and apply suitable measures to address them.

PART THREE

....

Information and knowledge silos

While one measure towards improved effectiveness should be to become data-informed when making project decisions, we need to ensure that the sources of information and knowledge are enabled and available. That means information and knowledge are produced, accessible and shared with the rest of the organization for other project teams to ingest into their decision-making.

Silos are created when information and knowledge are not shared across teams, forming barriers to information flow and collaboration.

To resolve this problem, most organizations maintain a knowledge management system. Here, employees and teams document information and knowledge, such as any elaborated solutions to particular problems, established processes and lessons learned, etc.

While common practice, the mere existence of a knowledge management system and its contents does not mean that information is shared. This is especially so in large organizations with many different domains and departments, such as IT with specialized groups for infrastructure, compliance, cybersecurity, etc. These groups rarely talk to each other, let alone actively share information.

Making information and knowledge available is not the same as sharing, even if it is encouraged. True sharing requires active communication and collaboration between teams and departments, while an organization's structure often only enables "on-demand" sharing. Some teams may be interested in a specific piece of information or insight and initiate broad and time-consuming research without knowing that such information is readily available within the organization and documented in a knowledge management system.

Hence, a knowledge or information silo happens when systems are disconnected by a lack of communication and collaboration. Documenting shareable information and knowledge is a prerequisite. However, teams and departments must communicate with each other, even if the information does not seem relevant to a current scope of work or project. That does not mean teams should get a detailed walkthrough of documented knowledge from each other, as this would be highly inefficient. More effective would be a frequent exchange between teams regarding their current work or the nature of their work. Some organizations organize brown bag sessions where a team or a department presents to a wider audience on the nature and purpose of their work. This kind of exchange leads to a better understanding of other departments, broadening views and eventually fostering collaboration and strengthening communication between teams.

Data scarcity

We often assume that insufficient data is available in the project management domain; hence many claim the need for a base of data from which to generate insights.

The truth is that there is usually plenty of data available across project teams in an organization. It's just that different business units may be unwilling to share their data, thus creating silos. This mentality is usually driven by a mindset of ownership and power. Whoever owns the data owns the power and is likely hesitant to share it with other groups.

It may take an update to an organization's rewards structure to incentivize different business functions to share data, generate insights and let other project teams recycle it.[1]

PART THREE

....

Insufficient transparency

Data analytics relies on the disclosure of knowledge and related artifacts in projects to make sense of it and provide accurate recommendations based on facts. Incomplete, or worse, incorrect data can result in incorrect results and insights and eventually misguide decision-making.

That means the availability of project data is important, as is its completeness and truthfulness, to understand what is going on in projects and make conclusions for future projects.

This can be a challenge in project management because (for often understandable reasons) project managers don't always tell the truth. The truth can be stretched by hiding certain elements that are sometimes decisive in the success of a project. Subtle lies can become second nature.

What is going on in your project?

Consider a typical scenario in projects. A steering committee meeting comes up and the material, including status reports, is prepared. The usual process is that it goes through multiple iterations to fine-tune the message, so stakeholders understand what is going on in a project. So far, so clear.

The problem is that fine-tuning often means inconvenient messages are dropped or downplayed, primarily because nobody wants to sound overly negative. When a project manager needs to communicate bad news, it is usually packaged so stakeholders hear something like this. "We have had a few hiccups here and there, which have impacted the timeline slightly, but we are fully on top of it, have taken measures XYZ, and are confident of getting back on track in a couple of weeks." In other words: "Don't worry, you can trust me."

In many cases, however, the truth looks more like this. "I made a mistake and underestimated the impact of a risk XYZ, therefore, we missed a major milestone. We have taken measures XYZ to get back on track which didn't work out. We'll check other options, and I am sure we'll come up with something which will work."

Would you be more confident in the project team's capabilities with the curated message or the truth? While curating messages is not a crime, in this case, the truth has turned into a lie.

You may wonder why many projects show up with a Green status in every reporting cycle, only to get into struggles and Amber or Red status shortly before the delivery date. The reason is that

> *Many project managers avoid speaking the truth.*

many project managers avoid speaking the truth. They would rather bend and stretch it because they don't want to appear incompetent. Perhaps they don't want to jeopardize a promotion. Perhaps they are overconfident that they can handle the issues while hiding as best they can. Eventually, that means the captured project data is either incomplete, inaccurate, or simply does not represent the truth. Such project data could result in inaccurate insights and wrong project decisions when used for analytics purposes.

Many project activities are hidden, as in the previous example where something was missed and corrective action was taken. All of this is undocumented because nobody wants to have to explain their failure.

When projects don't go as planned, the whole concept of data sharing is tested, because nobody likes to explain in detail why things ran to the wall. In the aftermath of a project failure, it's typically the project manager who must justify what happened. That often feels like being a defendant in a courtroom where you aim to be acquitted or try to reduce your sentence as much as possible. A post-mortem should capture precisely what went wrong.

But do those exercises uncover the whole truth in all its detail?

If you are a project manager, think about your frequent status reports. Is this the whole truth? Does it really show what is going on in the project? Not always.

Hidden realities

Hidden project activities are not necessarily about failures. Project managers often use their network and connections to peers to exchange favors.

Let's say a project manager needs approval from a change approval board (CAB) to deploy software to a productive environment, which may require some lead time depending on the organization and administrative practices. But this project manager may have a good friend in the CAB who could speed things up and help deliver the project faster.

The reality is that many project managers apply shortcuts in projects. It is a common and legitimate practice.

> *Nobody wants their shortcuts or failures exposed.*

Nobody wants their shortcuts or failures exposed, preferring to position themselves as the superhero who turns projects around, saves projects, and always delivers on promises. Naturally, we prefer to talk about our success stories rather than our failures. So when we fail or cheat to get something done, we'd rather hide it.

Here are a few scenarios that probably wouldn't get recorded in project artifacts and would lead to a distorted version of the truth:

- A project gets into a critical state and is at Red status based on newly identified risks. The project manager believes things are under control and has a reliable plan to bring it back on track. However, they prefer not to share it with stakeholders or sponsors as it would raise questions about how the project got to this point and potentially uncover failure by the project manager.

- A delivery timeline is completely overestimated, with an excessive contingency reserve to ensure plenty of time for delivery. The project manager justifies it with blunt lies, citing "technical complexity". When the project is delivered earlier, they emerge as a superhero.

- To the disadvantage of peers or stakeholders, the project manager intentionally hides information due to individual or political interests.

- Team members face ethical dilemmas and must choose between truth and loyalty. For example, they observe a superior's failure but don't raise or report it out of loyalty or fear.

- A project manager misses an important milestone. They rely on the favor of a related team or peer to make an exception to ensure that the missed milestone does not result in an overall delay in project delivery.

- A workaround is applied to carry out a project task faster and ensure that the project does not slip. However, the applied workaround violates company policies and, if uncovered, would result in disciplinary action against the project manager responsible.

These scenarios have one thing in common: valuable knowledge that would be explicit if properly disclosed and captured. More fundamental procedural problems could be identified and addressed instead of hidden practices becoming the norm. Effectively, hidden knowledge remains tacit and unshared.

If we want insights based on facts, we need to produce facts.

You might argue that applying data and analytics could uncover issues such as subtle lies and misaligned interests. But that would make it a kind of polygraph, triggering an alarm when a lie is detected. Data analytics should not be used to control and monitor people.

Analytics should help identify patterns in data, show emerging trends, and lead to actionable insights. It can show what we can't see through traditional means. But to work, data should represent what is going on in projects, beyond the high-level metrics of project milestones and financial targets.

If that is not the case, then analytics must deal with artifacts and information that hold half-baked truths and hidden failures. You might even call it fake news.

If we want insights based on facts, we need to produce facts.

Truth and transparency pave the way to a high-performing and evidence-driven project management practice. Failure is inevitable and should be embraced for the benefit of all project managers. The resulting learning enables progress and evolution.

Can you handle the truth?

A culture of truth, with full transparency and authenticity, has implications. It needs to support openness and honesty, where people can say things we might not want to hear. What if a team member questions your way of running a project and points out various weaknesses? Are you open to receiving this criticism?

Truth requires a mindset and culture that supports it.

....

Lack of knowledge-building

Proper project management knowledge and skills are key to delivering projects on time, within budget and scope, and providing the expected benefits. The question is how this knowledge and the necessary skills are applied, maintained and further developed across an organization.

As with any other discipline, people make mistakes, either due to a lack of competence or missing knowledge. Missing knowledge does not necessarily mean the person lacks appropriate project management education or the skills usually demonstrated through industry-leading certifications

When project teams work and experiment with unknowns, they build up knowledge.

such as Project Management Professional (PMP) or PRINCE2.[2,3]

Knowledge needs to evolve — especially in the project management domain. That evolution is based on applied practices and experiments, not academic and highly theoretical research. Projects are uncertain constructs that deliver unique products and services. Managers outline a delivery plan based on evolving knowledge and assumptions. When project teams work and experiment with unknowns, they build up knowledge.

Ineffective lessons

Delivering on time is crucial, especially in regulatory-driven industries where overrun timelines could noticeably impact an organization's finances or reputation. Timeframes are a vital element of a project schedule. What is often overlooked is that delivery involves more than providing a deliverable to the project customer, such as a developed software product or a constructed building. Lessons Learned is the opportunity to gain knowledge and insights from the project activities. Unfortunately, it is rarely baked into schedules.

Standard project management education recommends conducting a Lessons Learned session as part of project closure, to capture, review and document what went well and what didn't during the project's lifecycle. In many organizations, these sessions generate limited value due to various common problems.

Disengagement

The first issue is that people don't generally like meetings. A scheduled Lessons Learned feels like something to get through quickly. It's yet another meeting in an already crowded calendar. As a result, people show up disengaged, asking, haven't we delivered what was asked?

A project often feels like preparing to run the hundred-meter race at the Olympics. You train by doing the work and test it out through practice until delivery day at the Olympics. Once it's over and you've won, you have no motivation to go through some detailed walkthrough of what went well and what didn't. You are exhausted and far less engaged than before you crossed the finish line.

Hence a Lessons Learned meeting after the project feels like a burden. The result is that although people may be motivated to contribute to capturing the lessons, they are more likely driven by an attitude of 'Let's get it over with'.

Insufficient detail

Detailed insights can lead to learning. A software developer who experimented with various solutions to a coding problem may have identified a solution or method that would be helpful for future similar scenarios.

In my previous software development work, I usually explored ways of addressing particular problems. These contributed to my experience and helped me to improve, become more effective with coding, and efficient in terms of required effort. This could be valuable for other developers, helping them address similar problems better and faster. Such lessons and resulting learnings are often highly detailed, but sharing them is worthwhile for future projects.

While many organizations have implemented a culture of sharing insights and knowledge through appropriate documentation, projects often focus more on getting things done to complete delivery. When the time comes for a Lessons Learned session or retrospective, there is not always enough time for detail, meaning the lessons are superficial.

PART THREE

The blame game

The point of lessons learned is to do things better in the future. That, of course, implies that some things didn't go too well. Perhaps the communication between the IT team and a business change team was poor because of the change team's limited availability. This could be interpreted as a lack of commitment, and the team might be blamed for lower project performance. It's a common scenario, and although an experienced Lessons Learned facilitator can manage the situation, things can get tricky.

Chapter takeaways

- Sharing and distributing knowledge across the organization is crucial for a data-informed project management practice. A knowledge management system does not automatically prevent data and knowledge silos, as people are often unwilling to share data.

- Data and analytics rely on transparency, authenticity and people telling the truth to ensure transparency about what is really going on in projects. It requires a culture that promotes honesty, so people are willing to open up. Only then can we uncover inconvenient truths.

- Project environments often lack the proper building of knowledge. Although Lessons Learned is an established practice, if conducted ineffectively, people are not engaged, avoid necessary detail, and use it as a platform to determine blame.

CHAPTER NINE

Understanding Data

Before considering the transformation to a data-informed project management practice, we need to understand what data means in project management and delivery, and the value it can provide. Only then can we link the existing challenges and issues to effectively deliver projects and determine whether a transition would make sense.

Many people underestimate or completely miss this initial step. There is no single blueprint for such a transition as it depends on many factors specific to an organization, its structures, the capabilities of its people and their precise challenges.

A fundamental starting point is the awareness and understanding of data concepts, with a focus on project data.

....

Using data in projects

Data is a broad term, especially in the context of being "data-driven" or "data-informed." These terms emerged from the technological advances of big data and data analytics. Data is associated with information that is captured and stored in digital form, either in structured (e.g., databases, Excel sheets) or unstructured format (e.g., emails, videos).

The Cambridge Online Dictionary defines data as "Information, especially facts or numbers, collected to be examined and considered and used to help decision-making or information in an electronic form that can be stored and used by a computer."[1]

Data is not limited to information in electronic form; rather, as in the first part of the definition, it is collected information used to help decision-making. Just as decision-making didn't arrive with the digital age, data doesn't have to be digital.

Data is certainly nothing new in project management. As with many other disciplines, project management relies heavily on data and information to make decisions. Data and information can have various origins outside the digital domain, such as books, newspapers and magazines. It also comes from our observations, experience, education and intuition. All are sources of data that we process towards information and knowledge.

When you read a book or a magazine, you are consuming data and information that, consciously or not, can influence how you make decisions. Professional and personal experience form intuition and gut feelings that impact how you work and attack problems and solutions. For example, project managers use a lot of heuristics (rules of thumb) that were established based on identified patterns and deemed to work in certain scenarios. An example could be estimating testing activities in a software development project based on the required software development efforts, or calculating an appropriate contingency buffer to ensure a project is delivered by the targeted delivery date.

In his book *Gut Feelings*, Gerd Gigerenzer argues that gut feeling is a form of intelligence since one has to select the appropriate rule of thumb based on the environmental structures.[2] Intelligence is based on knowledge derived from information and data we process and make sense of.

Data has a lot to do with what is around us. It has been processed into information and turned into knowledge since project management was first established as a discipline.

As we said earlier, the human brain is constructed to forget things. When I recall one of my first projects as a project manager (a data migration project in a large organization), I can roughly remember the concepts we used, the challenges that we faced as a team, and some of the unique stories of craziness that sometimes happen in challenging projects. But I certainly couldn't provide a detailed stakeholder composition or the precise project milestones. Much of that is forgotten, but relevant elements that contributed to my experience as a project manager remain. You might hope to retrieve little details of your experience from the memory, but as Gerd Gigerenzer argues, "more memory is not generally better." Forgetting is a benefit as it enables our ability for abstraction, making human input and intelligence valuable in a data-informed practice.

> *Forgetting is a benefit as it enables our ability for abstraction, making human input and intelligence valuable in a data-informed practice.*

PART THREE

Where does project data come from?

Two crucial questions need answering about project data. Where does it come from? And how should we collect it to become data-informed?

Project data is readily available. We produce most of the data that is relevant for projects and their delivery during the lifecycle of a project. And we produce a lot of it — including data that you may not even label as data. That is because many people associate data with information that is computerized and captured digitally, such as Microsoft Word documents, emails, etc. Data does not have to be in digital format, although eventually, we want most of it digitized, to turn tacit into explicit knowledge wherever possible and enable it to get digitally processed towards valuable insights through analytics.

Figure 17: Examples of project management data

A selection of typically produced data artifacts in projects is shown in figure 17. Not all of these artifacts are necessarily available in digital format. In agile projects, you may remember physical Scrum or Kanban boards filled with Post-it notes (figure 18). Many shops still operate in this way, but most teams have switched to digital tools like Jira from Atlassian.

Figure 18: Agile board

We also produce data during project meetings by drawing things on a whiteboard or flipchart. It may be in a non-digital format, but that doesn't change its value. The following list includes examples of data artifacts that are usually produced and consumed within projects and are often only available in non-digital format:

- agile boards
- process diagrams
- mindmaps
- handwritten notes
- books
- handwritten meeting notes
- spoken word.

131

All these data artifacts hold some meaning for projects and will eventually influence decisions. Let's take the example of non-digital agile boards shown in figure 18. In a daily Scrum meeting, the team reviews the different tasks on the scrum board and may decide to readjust the priorities to meet the sprint goal based on the sprint progress.

Another example could be a team meeting where a mindmap is drawn on a whiteboard to elaborate the work breakdown structure and decide critical dependencies for the different work packages.

A further example is a Lessons Learned meeting where the various lessons are collected on Post-it notes and pinned on a wall. The outcome could be a decision on which actions address a particular lesson.

There are numerous other examples of non-digital data as, in the end, projects are run by people who interact outside of digital platforms, although this reduced immensely during the COVID-19 pandemic.

So data sources are more than just computer systems, folders and files. Given the value of non-digital data, such sources need to be considered when transitioning to a data-informed project management practice. One of the initial steps is to identify all data sources. That includes analyzing non-digital data sources and the possibility of digitizing to take full advantage of them.

Dark data is hidden value

When trying to identify the sources of data (and specifically relevant data that could lead us to valuable insights), we inevitably stumble across the concept of dark data.

This is data that is collected and stored but not used for any particular purpose, occupying storage and infrastructure. A typical example is system logs that are generated by IT systems, then not used again. These could be logs of employees entering the company building using access badges. The logs are maintained in case of an investigation into who entered the building and when, but most are never referred to.

There is also data that was created and used for a while. It may have had value, but then was no longer used. It is data that then sits idle and dark on company infrastructure.

And there is a lot of dark data. According to studies (including by IBM in 2018), it is estimated that eighty to ninety percent of all data in organizations is dark.[3] Storage is very cheap and most data is kept "just in case" — even though it will likely never be used.

But while the cost of storage might not be a problem, I'm concerned that dark data holds valuable but unused information for many business operations, including project management. Let's look at some examples to illustrate that.

Take a business meeting where we draw up thoughts, solutions and processes on a whiteboard. To capture this, we take pictures of the whiteboard with our mobile phones and upload the images to a Sharepoint folder. This way, we think we have stored valuable information which could probably help a specific audience, project, or business group. But it isn't stored or processed in a way that can provide lasting value and insights to an entire organization. That information goes dark.

The same is valid for other unstructured data, such as scanned documents, emails, notes and media files.

And then, there is project management data, such as project schedules, risk registers and stakeholder maps. Project management data often is only maintained and used for the duration of a project. When the project ends, data that has evolved into actual information and knowledge is usually stored in a project folder or on a local computer. Project management artifact data usually goes dark as it isn't looked at again.

Project management artifact data usually goes dark as it isn't looked at again.

Yet this data holds considerable value that could lead to decisive insights for future projects and other project teams, to learn from previous challenges, risks, issues, and other valuable information.

Dark data is like a hidden object that could provide value. Imagine you are in a library that is fully loaded with knowledge and information. If you want to learn about Asian cooking, you look up books that explain and teach it in detail and include recipes. Now, if the book you are looking for is in the wrong section, perhaps in banking, your search is handicapped. Eventually, you skip this part and rely on your basic cooking skills, filling the gaps with intuition and experimentation.

That is more or less how we've been operating in projects. We build up a lot of knowledge by creating a particular dish, and once we're done and have served it, we throw all our notes and knowledge into a random location where nobody can find it. Knowledge goes dark and is hidden.

Respect the data

We know that data is not new in project management. Project professionals consume and produce masses of it. Think of all the artifacts mentioned earlier, including project plans, schedules, risk registers, stakeholder maps, etc. Alongside those more common types, there is contextual data specific to the nature of projects (e.g., regulatory information in compliance projects, technical specifications for IT infrastructure projects, etc.).

While these are tangible artifacts, there is much more than that. For example, PowerPoint presentations that are used for steering committee meetings, drawings on whiteboards, scribbled notes in your notebook, emails, and even the spoken word between people in projects. All can be classified as data.

The importance is to examine your view of data in projects and become more mindful of it.

What do I mean by that?

Some years ago, I watched the TV show *Columbo* and recently rewatched some episodes. If you're unfamiliar with the series, Columbo was a police inspector (played by Peter Falk) who investigated tricky murder cases. What always fascinated me (and what I believe made the series so successful) is that Columbo solved seemingly perfect murder cases by mixing a highly analytical mindset with common sense. He questioned the obvious and put the puzzle together, piece by piece. Those puzzle pieces were his observations and the data he collected. For example, a weather report from last week, a car that was not wet although it was raining, and different cigarette brands in an ashtray. Many small pieces seemed unimportant, yet together they formed a picture that solved a murder case.

Essentially, Columbo paid attention to detail. He respected the minutiae, processed them with his intellect, used his experience to make sense of them, and came up with precise conclusions.

Transforming to a data-informed project management practice means becoming a Columbo, or a Sherlock Holmes, if you will. Respecting the detail means respecting the data. No matter how inconsequential it seems. The perception of something as straightforward and obvious is usually influenced by biased thinking.

It's like the optical illusion in figure 19. In this illustration, squares A and B appear to have different background colors, which is an illusion as they are the same. It shows how our brains trick us and impact our rational thinking. In this case, the brain processes the observation that square B is in shadow and therefore makes a correction of the shade, resulting in a perception that it is lighter than it is. This is reinforced by comparing square B to the squares next to it, which are also in shadow. But in reality, square A has exactly the same shade of grey as square B.

Figure 19: The checker shadow illusion, originally published by Edward H. Adelson[4]

We must be aware of our limitations and not disregard potential evidence just because it seems irrelevant. Although some data points could turn out to be so, the key is not to make an immediate judgment. Verify the data before disregarding it.

Verify the data before disregarding it.

That is especially true because single and isolated data points or pieces of information could appear useless, but they may provide meaning and generate new insights when aggregated.

Let's return to Columbo. It also pays to have an analytical mindset, make sense of different available details, and form a picture that gives meaning and leads to a solution and an answer to a question. For Columbo, the question was, "Who is the murderer?" His usual problem was alleged evidence or data points that combined to lay a false trail. But Columbo, with his sharp mind, applied human sense and intuition. He didn't believe in simple data points, so he added them together to make sense. In other words, data alone may not tell the truth, even though it is often regarded as fact. The truth is revealed when we combine information from data with human intellect. That's why data is an informant that supports managers in their decision-making.

Data is critical for project success

In previous chapters, I described the value of data and analytics, and the existing challenges of project teams to deliver projects effectively, confidently and consistently on time, on budget, and with the expected benefits. The question now is how data and analytics can address those challenges and improve project management.

PART THREE

Some people associate this with a first step towards introducing artificial intelligence, machine learning, robots and effectively a new intelligence that will take over the whole project delivery shop, making people's jobs obsolete. That translates into hesitation or disbelief that novel methods could benefit projects. Such thinking indicates a missing awareness, an ignorance of existing issues and challenges, and a resistance to progress and evolution.

Project management professionals will need to get comfortable employing data analytics as, sooner or later, intelligent technology will manage and deliver their projects. At that point, not using analytics in projects would be like competing against Lewis Hamilton in a Formula One race with a horse and carriage. Get real.

Plenty of dramatic stories should drive us to embrace new and innovative methods. Kodak's downfall came because they completely underestimated the digital age and what it meant for the film and photo industry. It wasn't that Kodak ignored digital capabilities; they simply acted out of fear that they could harm their existing business model and shied away from transforming and evolving their business. The rest is history.

Remember the introduction of spreadsheets? Dan Bricklin launched the first spreadsheet tool called VisiCalc. Soon, other spreadsheet applications hit the market, with the most popular one to date being Microsoft Excel. Spreadsheets highly impacted the accounting industry. Nowadays, no accountant would imagine doing their work by hand, but back then, many accountants were hesitant, fearing that these tools would make their jobs obsolete. And, to some extent, their fears were well-founded. Since 1980, around 400,000 accounting clerks have become obsolete as spreadsheets took over their role.

But spreadsheets made accounting more effective and easier, which resulted in 600,000 new jobs in the accounting industry.[5]

Of course, there will be changes in the project management domain, but it is a paradigm shift that professionals must embrace to stay competitive. It requires transformation and change.

As Caroline Carruthers and Peter Jackson rightly highlighted in their book *Data-driven Business Transformation*, transformation always involves risks. It is usually a painful exercise and often avoided.[6]

That sounds ironic when we want to transform and change project management; a domain whose primary reason for existence is change and transformation. You might expect project and change management professionals to be comfortable. But there is a difference between changing and being changed, between transforming and being transformed. Resistance, hesitation and doubt appear as much here as anywhere. It takes great leadership to steer people through transformation.

Projects generate high-value fuel

Applying data analytics in projects requires data. It is fuel for a modern engine that uses analytics to produce new insights. But we already know that the first questions are usually "What data are we talking about?" and "Where is it coming from?" The answers depend on what we want to achieve.

Amazon and Netflix need data about their customers — their shopping habits and navigation history — to get insights into customer behavior and help them find products they want.

In risk management, compliance departments in banks collect data from third-party sources, such as public watchlists, social media profiles and news articles, to build customer profiles, including their digital footprint.

So, what are we trying to achieve in project management? Given that many projects don't meet their defined targets, the goal should be to improve the accuracy of forecasts, estimates, risk assessments and project decisions in general.

A starting point is assessing past projects' performance, overruns, successes and failures. We can retrieve plenty of information from project management data and related artifacts, such as project schedules, stakeholder maps, risk management plans, and elsewhere. If we keep collecting and analyzing those artifacts, we should clearly understand what is going on.

Projects can benefit a lot from the data that projects produce, but that doesn't mean third-party data isn't useful. It definitely could be. But the main source of project data that will produce new insights is the already generated, day-in and day-out, within projects.

If produced and maintained correctly, such data can provide immense value to help a practice continuously grow and progress by learning from the past, running analytics across relevant project management data, and producing insights that we might otherwise miss.

Many people think that projects are such unique constructs that they cannot be mapped onto other projects. I cannot emphasize enough that this is incorrect.

Projects produce unique products or services, often by applying established processes and solutions. Like building a house, the same processes and tasks create very different end products and new knowledge.

New demands lead to a new mix of identified elements retrieved from experience and novelty that gets explored and elaborated using skills. Combining replicable experiences, refining and improving them, and exploring novel elements produces new knowledge, leading to a unique product or service.

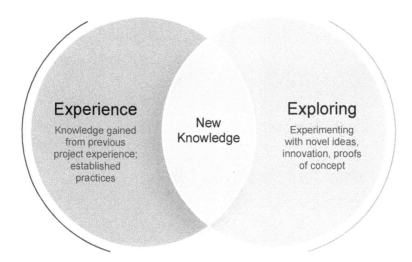

Figure 20: Projects generate new knowledge

From data to wisdom

Let's look at how data transforms from cryptic to knowledge that generates value.

I got into computer programming in my teenage years and started by learning two programming languages, BASIC and Turbo Pascal, that were popular at the time. A programming language is simply a set of instructions and strings translated into machine code for a computer to understand and execute. Equally, when we want to understand what a computer program is doing, the underlying machine code (a sequence of 0s and 1s or hexadecimal code as in figure 21) is translated into a computer programming language.

Figure 21: Hexadecimal code

I always wondered how someone could read and make sense of machine code. Perhaps some hardcore machine code programmers can, but I think it looks cryptic and impenetrable. Data in its raw format is useless; it requires processing and translation. Translating machine code into a programming language gives meaning and context to unreadable data, so we can properly understand it.

Similarly, in projects, data may be a bunch of numbers representing an effort estimate for a particular activity or task in the project plan. Or a financial figure that is part of a project budget calculation. The number alone does not make sense until we know what it refers to. It needs to be processed and transformed into something that adds meaning and context.

Clive Humby, the British mathematician and data science entrepreneur behind the popular phrase "Data is the new oil", elaborated further. He says oil is "valuable, but if unrefined it cannot be used. It has to be changed into gas, plastic, chemicals, to create a valuable entity that drives profitable activity; so must data be broken down and analyzed for it to have value."[7]

In the same way, data is processed to provide value. The following commonly acknowledged DIKW model (figure 22) describes the different stages of turning raw data into value-providing knowledge and wisdom.

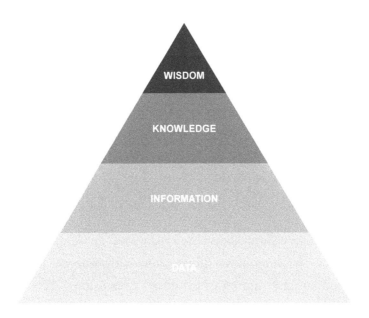

Figure 22: DIKW model

Let's unpack these stages of transformation in more detail.

Data

Data simply stands for facts and figures. Data alone may not be of value, especially when it comes to unstructured data, such as video or image information, emails, etc. Such information must be processed and structured to extract value. We have to turn data into information.

In projects, an isolated number could represent an estimate for a work item, but it is meaningless until we know what it belongs to.

Information

Information is data that is processed and organized. It is structured and provides meaning which improves the reliability of the data, ensuring understandability and ultimately reducing uncertainty. This could include project plans, risk registers, financial project information, etc.

Knowledge

Information alone may not provide context for what we are looking at. Imagine taking over a project and inheriting all those project artifacts. You have to put everything into context. You might read a project schedule, but how do certain risks impact the schedule? How do project costs map onto line items in the schedule or work breakdown structure? We need to connect the dots to get context, and to add context, we transform information into knowledge.

Knowledge takes information and provides an understanding of the subject. It combines information with human experience, understanding and intuition to draw conclusions. We have an understanding, connect the dots and act on it.

PART THREE

An example could be a conclusion that, based on past performance and expected delivery dates, we need to ramp up the team with additional senior-level software engineers, expertise, and sufficient experience in a specific programming language, such as Java, Python and C++.

Wisdom

Wisdom is essentially about applying relevant, proven knowledge. While knowledge is derived from the collection of information, wisdom comes from the collection of knowledge. This is usually the scope of a project management centre of excellence (PMCoE) to use the accumulated knowledge from a wider range of projects, identify patterns of challenges, and take action to update project management frameworks or make new advanced tools available to project teams.

Wisdom, therefore, relies on accumulated knowledge. The emphasis is on *accumulated* as we need to look at the sum of knowledge gained over time from projects to identify patterns and get true insights. But one of the key problems is that knowledge often is not sustained, shared, or maintained.[8]

For example, looking at projects of similar nature and with the same characteristics, and identifying patterns of discrepancies to meet a cost target, could help with reviewing existing estimates and/or estimation techniques to make project cost planning exercises for such projects more realistic.[9]

Brian O'Driscoll, an Irish former professional rugby player, once said: "Knowledge is knowing that a tomato is a fruit. Wisdom is knowing not to put it in a fruit salad."[10]

That is certainly a great way to look at it because gaining knowledge is relatively easy. In project management, you need the skill to put things into context, like understanding that your project is understaffed or at risk of not meeting a milestone. Many people gain knowledge in project management by taking training classes, getting certified, and so on. But wisdom is about retaining knowledge gained over time, making sense of it as a whole, and taking action.[11]

Wisdom is about retaining knowledge gained over time.

This is why wisdom is strongly linked to experience and intuition. Given we usually forget a lot of knowledge over time, our strength is not memory. Remember that is not necessarily a bad thing. This weakness enables our ability for abstraction while data and analytics can help us to keep the memory alive.

Chapter takeaways

- Project management produces large amounts of data in both digital and non-digital formats. Making use of it means adopting the mindset of an investigator and recognizing the limitations and handicaps of data as well as human logic and understanding.

- Dark data is collected but hidden and not used again. Plenty of valuable data, including artifacts like project schedules and risk logs, go dark once a project is over, reducing and limiting data and analytics capabilities.

- Data in its raw format is useless. It needs to be transformed into information and knowledge for proper use. Wisdom comes from making sense of accumulated knowledge and identified patterns.

PART THREE

PART FOUR
Behavior: Enabling Enhanced Knowledge

*"The problem isn't really change, it's whether
two people change in the same direction."*

— Shaun Murphy

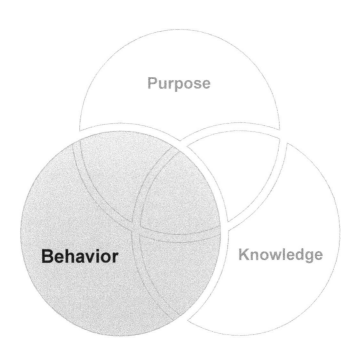

CHAPTER TEN

Recognize Your Limitations

Project management relies mostly on people. Their experience, expertise and skills are important factors for the successful outcome of a project. But leaders know that teams must be cohesive to perform at their best. People's behaviors and resulting culture are crucial in successfully delivering change.

Accordingly, organizations often take relevant initiatives to make people's behaviors work for organizational success. Initiatives to drive engagement, motivation and commitment, remove silos and change workplace design are all useful.

Yet several blockages in our thinking and behaviors hinder our attempts to deliver successful project outcomes.

In this chapter, we will shine a light on those gaps. Our primary goal is to become fully aware of them and recognize the limitations of traditional human-driven ways. That helps us understand the real problem behind what is stopping us from getting projects consistently across the finish line.

We will briefly review common factors that lead to gaps in the project management space:

- misinterpreting information or signals
- flawed and ill-informed project decisions
- fake knowledge
- myopia.

....

Beware the illusion of knowledge

Daniel Boorstin, an American historian at the University of Chicago, noted that "the greatest enemy of knowledge is not ignorance, but the illusion of knowledge."[1] By nature, humans struggle to deal with limited information, so we often treat it as complete. When we realize there's an information gap, we build a suitable story to make available information believable.

Steven Sloman and Philip Fernbach elaborated extensively on this effect in their book *The Knowledge Illusion.* They highlighted that most of what we think we know is just a bunch of associations and links between abstract snippets of information.[2]

There is no way of knowing every detail of everything, yet we often have to make decisions based only on a high-level understanding of a subject. Most of what we refer to as knowledge is simply strongly held beliefs.

Recognizing this should help us avoid making hasty conclusions just because we think "This is straightforward", or "We know that this works" or other dangerous statements.

PART FOUR

Consistent messages drive knowledge illusion

What drives an illusion of knowledge? It's when we hear something often and pick up a particular message or statement. The more we hear it, the more our belief of knowing something grows, even if there is no credible evidence and the belief is no more than an assumption. Repeatedly hearing a specific message can lead us to misinterpret the frequency of a message as fact and not bother seeking genuine evidence.

In Chapter One, I described how Cambridge Analytica manipulated people's voting behavior by exposing people to targeted online campaigns. They were flooded with consistent messages that drove them to vote a particular way in the election.

Similarly, we hear some rules and standards in project management so often that we don't question them.

I once heard a junior project manager provide an initial cost estimate for a project, then add fifteen percent for project management efforts. When asked how he got to this figure, he didn't know but said, "Everybody uses fifteen percent for any project." In another discussion, the same project manager said he applies the agile methodology to all his projects. He said he wasn't familiar with any other methodology, and that the organization supported and communicated the view that projects can only be successful using Agile. I was shocked as such conformity to rules and messages is counterproductive and plain wrong.

It is an example of where behaviors are impacted and reinforced by the environment. An environment or a culture that is not evidence-driven

PART FOUR

and does not validate information reinforces a message, and the actors turn their initial assumptions into outright belief and knowledge.

Knowledge is justified by true belief

Evidence and facts are important. Yet *holding* evidence and facts does not necessarily mean we *know* the facts. Belief by the person holding the facts and evidence is essential. There must be familiarity with the subject and an ability to interpret and consume the facts. Factual competence enables belief as figure 23 describes.

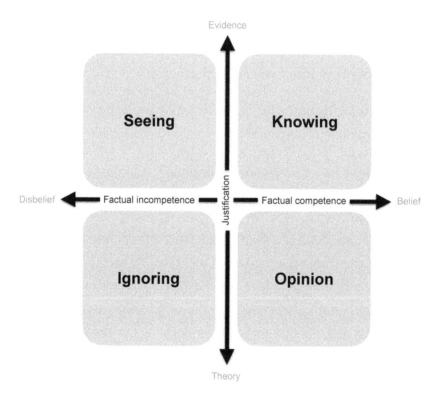

Figure 23: Knowledge needs belief

It's like the offside rules in soccer. You may see where a player is standing, but unless you are familiar with rules, you can't possibly know the player was offside.

Knowing requires justification and true belief enabled by related subject matter expertise.

Know what we believe or believe what we know

Failing to believe something precludes knowing it. Facts are readily referred to as knowledge because facts are deemed to be true.

If we didn't believe in facts, we wouldn't seek to prove them and make them part of our knowledge. We prefer to exclude and question such facts, even if they are proven elsewhere. Confidence in facts means understanding them, which enables us to look for evidence. Here are some examples.

- The mathematical formula of $1+1=2$ is a fact that is known to be true. But we only know it because we learned about it in school. We gained belief through learning and understanding, and added it to our knowledge when we generated the scientific evidence for it.
- The existence of an unknown planet XYZ might be a fact. We only come to know if we have actual belief and confidence about its existence, and seek and find evidence for it.

Cognitive rigidity

Facts, evidence and beliefs build knowledge and expertise. As in the previous example, consistently allocating fifteen percent for project management efforts in a cost estimate might be evidenced and appropriate. Project managers apply numerous rules-of-thumb

PART FOUR

or mental models in their day-to-day work. And the more often and longer these are applied, the stronger the belief that they are fundamental and undeniable knowledge. It leads to what psychologist Gary Klein calls cognitive rigidity.[3] When confronted with evidence that may prove a particular method wrong, people hold on to their beliefs and even disregard the new information, explaining that the data may be flawed or of low quality.

When using data and analytics in projects, there are risks that, unconsciously, evidence is downplayed and not taken seriously. It is linked to the status quo bias, a behavior characterized by statements such as "It always worked this way, so why should we change it".

But evolution, progress and improvement are only possible with change. Inevitably it requires the ability to unlearn. As the American futurist Alvin Toffler wrote decades ago, "The illiterate of the 21st century will not be those who cannot read and write, but those who cannot learn, unlearn and relearn".[4]

....

Towards informed decisions

Project managers constantly make decisions, ranging from what meetings we should hold within the project team, to the communication channels and where we store project artifacts. The type of methodology we should use (Agile, Waterfall) is based on the kind of project we're working on. We decide on suitable delivery methods and how we evaluate risks and issues. And on it goes.

We negotiate with stakeholders, coming to agreements and decisions. Our day-to-day work is packed with decisions. Decision-making is at the core of project management. Yet the skill is often underestimated. We rely on the right interpretation of information and the skill to determine the consequences of decisions. It is vital for project outcomes.

Information means any relevant input that helps assess the options and the attached risks. It means we gather and make sense of facts and information from various sources, leading to different ideas and decision options.

As every option has a particular risk and an expected benefit, informed decision-making means assessing and comparing the risks and benefits. A typical example of informed decision-making is when you hire a new project team member, say a business analyst, you collect profiles of potential candidates, review their CVs, interview them, and collect their professional references.

Decision quality

In project management, many decisions are of poor quality, which can have a devastating impact. We see these results in the increasing number of project failures.

How do we usually make decisions? In the worst case, they are impulsive, perhaps because we need to decide quickly. These decisions are the opposite of informed, and the outcomes are often poor or even wrong.

To improve the quality of a decision, we should hear opinions from other team members.

PART FOUR

Mostly, however, decision-making is made in a group, a project steering committee or the project team. To estimate tasks in agile environments, we use techniques such as planning poker.

The quality of a decision certainly improves with group consensus, although we may miss out on important information available from data and evidence-based practices (see figure 24). Biases play a huge role in decision-making, and while we may think that group consensus should address this issue, it's not necessarily true.

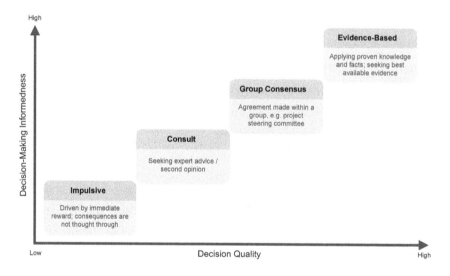

High

Decision-Making Informedness

Evidence-Based
Applying proven knowledge
and facts; seeking best
available evidence

Group Consensus
Agreement made within a
group, e.g. project
steering committee

Consult
Seeking expert advice /
second opinion

Impulsive
Driven by immediate
reward; consequences are
not thought through

Low   Decision Quality   High

Figure 24: Improving decision quality

In group settings, we often see the phenomena known as groupthink, which is where individual thinking is lost just to reach a consensus. It's like adopting uniformity to comply with the majority view. Such behavior also changes risk tolerance as people are less risk-averse in groups than as individuals.

To raise the decision quality and become truly informed in our decision-making, we need to use data and facts, and apply an approach that leverages data and its insights.

Bounded rationality

A common constraint to effective decision-making is bounded rationality. That means getting to a decision that satisfies the need but is not necessarily the best or optimal. The concept is based on three specific limitations:

Cognitive limitations

Decision-makers have limited analytical and computational abilities. Given this limitation and their inability to make a perfect judgment based on information, they make wrong judgments.

Biases usually kick in with subjective opinions. It's an illusion to think our opinions are carefully screened for biases. Opinions are subjective views that are impacted by our natural cognitive biases and personal interests.

> *It's an illusion to think our opinions are carefully screened for biases.*

Appendix B lists a selection of biases that are common in projects. These cognitive biases often affect project decisions and could result in wrong decisions, cost or schedule overruns, and even project failures.

Information imperfection

Decision-makers do not have access to all the information relevant to a decision. In the age of big data, it is not humanly possible to collect

PART FOUR

and process all the pertinent information. That means decision-makers always will have only a subset or sample of all available information, and often that sample is unrepresentative or flawed.

In this context, let's revisit the four categories of Knowns and Unknowns made prominent by Donald Rumsfeld. He suggested there are known knowns, known unknowns, unknown knowns, and unknown unknowns.[5]

Known knowns

Known knowns are knowledge that is confirmed and helps towards an optimal decision.

An example is line items in project plans. We consider these tasks and activities confirmed and validated in terms of suitability and effort. Let's say your project plan for a construction project has an estimated and scheduled line item for plumbing work. As this can be planned, known and confirmed, it is perfect information.

Known unknowns

These are assumptions that cannot be confirmed. In a construction project, we know that atmospheric conditions can change and impact our schedule, but we cannot predict the weather.

Unknown knowns

This is unknown information that is known to someone — but not necessarily to the decision-maker. This can happen when a project team has relevant information about the required efforts and costs of a particular technical solution in an engineering project. If that information is not shared with other projects and a decision-maker is unaware, then it is hidden information.

Unknown unknowns

And then there are factors that we don't know we don't know. In Chapter Five, we discussed Black Swans, which are major impact events that are entirely unforeseeable. Earthquakes are an example. Another more tangible example is the harmful effects of cigarettes, which used to be an unknown unknown, as we were unaware of their negative impact for many years after they were introduced. But further research made it clear that cigarettes are harmful to health, so eventually it turned into a known known. With what we know now, many people would never have started smoking.

Information imperfection is primarily linked to those two categories of unknown knowns and unknown unknowns as there is a significant lack of information for project managers to make an informed assessment. And that is what we refer to as uncertainty.

For project risks that fall into the categories of known unknowns and known knowns, we have more or less information available to quantify and properly assess them.

The bucket of unknown knowns (uncertainty) has increased as a flow-on from the exponential growth of data. We sit in an ocean of data but consume only a mouthful.

We sit in an ocean of data but consume only a mouthful.

Risk myopia

We are left with a reduced view of project risks. The term for this is risk myopia, introduced by David Hillson, who is known as the Risk Doctor. He argues that many project professionals focus too much on short-term risks and ignore long-term strategic risks. That means they are missing out on the full risk picture. Such symptoms lead to a limited perspective on project risks by being too short-sighted.

While we can remediate gaps in a risk management approach, the exponential growth of data and information leads to short-sightedness. The amount of data needing to be analyzed and used for project management to ensure decent coverage of risks goes way beyond our human processing capabilities. In today's projects, we use and process only a small subset of available information. The rest goes to the bucket of uncertainty and leaves us crippled in risk management and forecasting. For a more detailed explanation, I recommend David Hillson's book *The Risk Doctor's Cures for Common Risk Ailments*.[6]

Forecasting and predicting are not in our nature

We could use some help here. Project management is about forecasting future events, planning tasks and activities, their duration, predicting and evaluating any possible constraints, and making related decisions to steer the project to a successful conclusion. But, ironically, these are where project managers are consistently bad and fail.

Humans are dominated by cognitive biases and overly optimistic thinking. Daniel Kahneman and Amos Tversky introduced this theory in 1979, suggesting that people tend to underestimate the time, costs and risks of future activities and tasks while overestimating the benefits of the same activities.[7,8] We are naturally too optimistic, commonly described as an optimism bias. And even when fully aware of this limitation in ourselves, we still fall for it.

It is one of the key reasons why so many projects are underestimated, risks incorrectly evaluated, and deadlines or budget targets missed, even though experience tells us we should know better. Several prominent examples are a testament to this kind of behavior.

- The Olympic Games (no event has ever been delivered on budget)[9]
- Germany's Berlin-Brandenburg airport construction (overran the project schedule by nine years)[10,11]
- FIFA's Football World Cup in Brazil in 2014 (total stadium cost was exceeded by approximately US$1bn)[12,13]

While project failures usually have a series of reasons, the dominating factor remains the overly optimistic view of project planners. Wrong estimates lead to wrong decisions and highly optimistic plans.

We carry out several critical project management tasks that we are innately awful at, such as estimating. Our natural abilities and intelligence are designed to think more conceptually and strategically. Instead, we spend too much time on activities that natural incompetence says we shouldn't.

We spend too much time on activities that natural incompetence says we shouldn't.

PART FOUR

Would you try to fly without assistance? Have you ever thought, "If birds can fly, I probably can, too"? No, neither have I.

Why?

Because human beings are not designed to fly like birds. We do not have that ability, but we wanted to get around faster, so after many attempts with mounted wings (figure 25), we eventually took advantage of technology and invented the aeroplane.

Figure 25: Otto Lilienthal's flying glider

In project management, we do many things people are not designed for, so we frequently fail. The key is to learn from our failures, recognize our limitations, and explore other ways to enhance our capabilities.

PART FOUR

Decision time

Another growing challenge is that decision-makers often do not have enough time to make quality decisions. And time-poor environments suggest there will be less and less time available to do so. When decisions need to be taken immediately or in a very short timeframe, there's no room for much analysis or consulting. This is illustrated in figure 26.

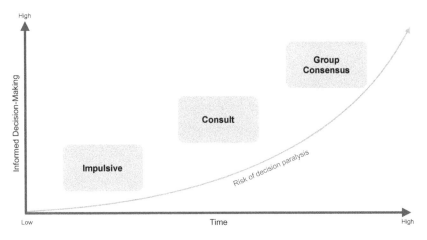

Figure 26: Decision time

Many project managers often hesitate to make decisions and fall into the trap of analysis paralysis, stretching the time to come up with a decision. They keep over-analyzing the same information without arriving at a decisive conclusion. By the time a decision is taken, that information might already be obsolete.

COVID-19 has demonstrated this, with the shift to working-from-home taking place almost overnight. Quick decisions were taken to try out new digital platforms or infrastructure and set things up, so organizations could continue to operate. Some measures failed, and

PART FOUR

some required rework, or adjustment, all while organizations still needed to operate effectively.

But the point is that new information comes in and may change things very fast. We do not know things until we know them. The earlier we get our hands on relevant information, the faster we can react. The more time we spend considering, the more difficult it is to solve a problem or issue. You can see the impact of delays in figure 27.

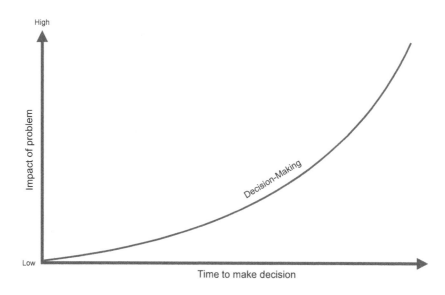

Figure 27: Impact of delayed decisions

Think about negotiations with a vendor to use their services for a project. The longer it takes to come to a decision and an agreement, the more progress is impacted. If the project business case has a time factor, a deliverable will be required by a specific time to accomplish the project benefits. In such a case, a decision delay could mean that the business case has changed, requiring new measures, other services, and other agreements.

Given this dilemma, managers often select the first option that is good enough.

Imagine you have to put a project team together, but with limited time to get things started, you fear you may overrun the project timeline. So you choose the first available candidates who appear to meet the project needs. You may choose people you know, have worked with before and trust, even though they may not be the best choice. You rule out other candidates as you do not have enough time. The decision here is not very informed as there hasn't been enough analysis of all possible alternatives.

On the other hand, you know there never will be the right amount of information.

To solve suboptimal decision-making, the theory of bounded rationality suggests that decision-makers must be willing to adapt their rational approach. For example, they must determine how much information is reasonable to pursue during the information-gathering stage; they cannot reasonably expect to gather and analyze all possible information.

Going beyond 'good enough'

There's a common understanding that gathering more information means we make more informed decisions, thus reducing uncertainty. This can result in searching for all potentially relevant information and data, which goes beyond what people can rationally process.

More information increases complexity while not necessarily adding to decision quality. Seeking more information often is misused to win time and delay a decision, arguing that it improves decision-making

What was meant to reduce uncertainty may have the opposite effect.

quality. In this information age, we think we are lucky because the quantity of information should make our decision-making more accurate.

However, what was meant to reduce uncertainty may have the opposite effect because we get distracted by additional data points and increasing complexity. It also means that our aim to get closest to certainty will likely end in greater uncertainty.

Figure 28: The overload problem
(Image credits: nikolpetr/Shutterstock.com)

A typical example of an apparent overload problem is traveling during the summer holiday season — especially if you have small kids who refuse to go on holiday without their entire toy collection.

A short one- or two-week getaway to sit on a beach involves enough luggage for a six-month roundtrip through an entire continent. Only to realize you forgot your snorkeling gear because you were distracted trying to squeeze too many clothes into your suitcase.

Taking more than you need is an effort to increase the chances of a fantastic vacation and reduce uncertainty. But that approach creates a distraction, and you end up forgetting important and relevant things.

Here's another example. Imagine you are a professional writer wanting to buy a new computer. You have specific requirements for features that support your work. Perhaps you focus on which applications come with the computer, the user-friendliness and the keyboard layout. Maybe you want dictation functions. With all the relevant information gathered, you should have all the information necessary to make a decision. But you are undecided and explore all the additional features. You find out about multimedia and gaming capabilities, built-in cameras and touchscreens. That all sounds great and maybe you'll use them sometime, so you look for more brands and products to consider.

Your search for additional information delays the decision and distracts you from your original criteria. You may make a detailed comparison of built-in webcams — even though that functionality is unimportant for your original purpose.

Seeking more information is based on the assumption that additional information and clarification will improve your decision-making

PART FOUR

quality. But such an approach may contribute to project risk as it costs time.

The term *information overload* has become popular in recent years as digital transformation and the exponential increase in data have given us easy and fast access to an ocean of information. But information overload is not something to fight against because we have created it. It is effectively a failure to filter information in the analysis, and let go of the FOMO (Fear of missing out) syndrome.

Information is important, and we need it to make informed decisions. But be aware of a few obvious, yet often forgotten, aspects:

1. **You'll never be able to gather enough information**. You could search forever and end up going around in circles. New information is constantly being created, leading to new links and dependencies. Whatever information we hold will never be enough and we'll keep looking for those missing pieces.

2. **Analyze the information that you have, and stop focusing on looking for more data**. Often, we have enough relevant information to make a call, but we procrastinate because we don't think we know enough to make a decision. Focus on your goals and stick to them by asking the right questions. Does a piece of information likely have the answer to any of your focused questions? If yes, that's great. Otherwise, disregard that information. Filtering is the key.

3. **Don't just rely on data**. The best source of relevant information is usually ourselves, derived from our experience and intuition. Too often, though, we think information needs to come from elsewhere — from the internet or other experts. Yet if you know of a working solution from past projects that

could be useful, why do you need extra information? The downside of the information age is that we underestimate our experience, intuition and intelligence, and overestimate data.

The cure, if one exists, starts with an awareness that certainty is an illusion, especially when making decisions about future events. For data-informed decision-making, the best decisions come from a combination of experience, intuition and filtered information. Effectively, there is no such thing as information overload. Problems usually arise from how we deal with information and our inability to make sense of information.[14]

> *There is no such thing as information overload.*

....

Cultural constraints

How information is processed and curated for informed decision-making has a lot to do with organizational culture, especially when people's behaviors, current practices, and habits need adjustments to make a data-informed project management practice work. Much existing literature highlights the importance of culture in the context of project management and delivery.

Edgar Schein of MIT's Sloan School of Management is recognized for his research and work regarding organizational culture. He defined culture as "the pattern of basic assumptions that a given group has invented, discovered, or developed in learning to cope with its problems of external adaptation and internal integration."

PART FOUR

171

Schein suggests that culture can be considered the primary source of resistance to change.[15]

This implies that the successful implementation of organizational change (essentially what projects aim to achieve) is highly influenced by an organization's culture.

Given a project is an organizational construct (albeit temporary), project culture represents the shared values, norms and beliefs of a project team and organization. It shapes team members' behaviors, adherence to standards, rules and best practices, and how they collaborate.

Many project teams loosely follow defined guidelines. Others have the flexibility to define their own ways of working within an overarching project management framework (primarily in agile-driven organizations), while specific formalized rules are strictly followed and mandated across the organization for consistency (e.g., production deployment procedures for software applications).

Schein's organizational culture model highlights basic assumptions shared by project team members. These are effectively deeply embedded, intangible and unconscious behaviors that are usually developed over a longer period. Given the importance of culture and required behaviors toward a data-informed and evidence-based project delivery practice, one of the most important aspects of a successful transition is to conduct an initial assessment of existing behaviors of project teams to determine their impact and potential to block progress, innovation and growth.

Changing established behaviors and beliefs, and bringing in data and analytics that would unmask discrepancies and shortfalls in people's day-to-day work certainly doesn't sound too appealing. It feels like people have a watchdog beside them, monitoring whether they are doing their work correctly. That makes the cultural aspect so important in this whole journey. It is all about letting go of old patterns of thinking, habits and how we deal with information.

There might be reluctance in some cases, as disclosing detailed information and data could reveal failure. When projects fail, there is naturally less willingness to share project data and information, as they are often associated with the failure of the project manager.

You see, then, that becoming data-informed in projects requires considering several aspects of behavior and culture. We take measures to drive data, analytics, experience, expertise and intuition in a balanced and well-tuned interplay that generates the best possible and most effective knowledge and project intelligence.

Sharing data is delicate, especially when it is linked to project failures. It requires trust and an environment that rewards rather than leads to punishment. We need to accept that by sharing data from failures, we put aside ego and contribute to improving the entire project management shop. The threat of punishment means nobody shares truthful data. Instead, they offer the bare minimum, tweaked, so they don't show up as failing project managers.

It is like sharing project plans with your external vendor. Before doing so, you make sure that anything that is sensitive or confidential to the company is removed. You disclose the bare minimum they need to know and nothing more.

Bringing data and analytics into the project management space requires a culture of openness that allows failure and doesn't transmit a message that will make people hide or stay silent rather than speak up.

> *Too often, project failures are associated with incompetence.*

Too often, project failures are associated with incompetence, although, in many cases, it is the project organization, culture, or missing support from senior management that drives projects into failure. We must allow people to point to inconvenient truths without being punished.

I have seen projects where a demanding and micro-managing project sponsor requested detailed status updates every week in a specific senior-management-like format. Since the sponsor was generally feared, several people dedicated at least a full day per week to putting together a status report and running it through reviews, editing and formatting. All to please the sponsor and keep him happy. A full day of project work was wasted on this every week, while the same sponsor pushed for the fast delivery of the project. Yet, nobody spoke up because of fear.

Wasted knowledge

Much of the quantitative information produced in project management is worth sharing with other project teams. Earlier I suggested that treating valuable project artifacts like waste and throw-away products is a barrier to an effective data-informed project management practice. You might imagine setting up relevant processes and rules would be sufficient to change those behaviors and make people store and retain project data. But we need transparency and openness beyond storing documents in the right folder. Sharing and maintaining knowledge should accompany the *active sharing* of tacit qualitative knowledge.

Establishing a sharing culture means understanding that it is a win for everyone. Sharing data and knowledge improves the performance of other projects and drives improvement for an entire project management department and its overall performance.

Resolving data silos and uncovering dark data is the right thing to do, but it doesn't prevent wasted knowledge unless people have fully bought into a sharing culture.

Stubbornness

Managers are often driven by a stubbornness that originates from various motivations. This is evident in the attitudes of people who favor a specific approach and claim there is no better way.

For instance, the introduction of agile methodologies caused some people to become agilists who believe traditional methods are useless and obsolete, while others think traditional methods are the only ones that work.

Some people rely totally on guidelines and bodies of knowledge provided by project management associations like the Project Management Institute (PMI), International Project Management Association (IPMA), or Association for Project Management (APM), seeing those as precise instructions on how to manage and run projects.

Flexibility and openness about techniques, processes and methodologies are essential to running projects effectively. The discipline of project management relies on learning and evolution.

PART FOUR

Claiming that one method or technique is the only way indicates a fixed mindset and a sort of stubbornness that is counterproductive and a block to progress and development.

There are other sources of stubbornness too. These arise in people who have not received a proper project management education, yet claim a deep understanding of how to run projects. Often you'll find senior managers in an organization who are experts in a particular business domain. They get involved in a change initiative and become project sponsors, based on their rank and seniority. But instead of becoming educated on the discipline of project management, they see their seniority, rank and role as providing a position from which to direct, guide and educate project managers. This can happen even if the project manager has had a formal project management education and proper experience.

This stubbornness can have a ripple effect across cultural barriers. When senior managers indicate they don't need to be educated by people with greater expertise but lower rank, then people are muted. People who identify issues in their directions may not speak up for fear of punishment for challenging a senior manager's way.

Traditional thinking

An essential element of project management practices is developing new methods and techniques to meet the demands of projects that change in nature, speed and complexity according to the evolution of business environments.

It is interesting, though, that many people in project management get busy fighting Agile wars. They argue that one flavor of Agile is better than another, condemning other methodologies, including traditional Waterfall methods.

Supporters of older methods are often labeled old-fashioned and traditionalists, but I think traditional thinking has nothing to do with preferring one method or technique over the other. Thinking that blocks progress is characterized by being too fixed on a single way of running projects, no matter which methodology.

Do you see the paradox? So-called agilists who call supporters of Waterfall "traditionalists" and claim Agile as the only method, are themselves traditional thinkers because they are stuck in their thinking, blocking progress and innovation in projects.

No methodology can or should dominate. The best results from projects come with a variety of methodologies and ideas. Diversity is key. It is up to the project manager to choose the right methodology for the nature and needs of a given project. In the end, one is not better than another; it all depends on what is best for a project.

We need to let go of traditional thinking, or we risk developing prejudiced opinions and disabling the value of data and analytics. It's like eating your favorite food day in and day out, without any variety. You'd get sick of it after a while.

Diversity of opinion, methodologies and knowledge is the key to progress, and evolving project management methods and delivery approaches.

Natural stupidity

Many articles, books and research papers examine project outcomes; however, there is no clear agreement on what defines success or

PART FOUR

failure. It is fair to say that it depends on what has been agreed in a project.

Stupidity in project management usually comes into play when project stakeholders ignore the fact that projects cannot guarantee a successful outcome. That's because projects are about the future, which no-one can predict with absolute certainty. Projects are also sometimes treated as vehicles detached from uncertainty and complexity — practically anything labeled as VUCA. These seem to ignore the practice of risk management completely. Research shows stakeholders often expect project teams to "do the same thing again but with a different outcome".[16]

Project managers often respond to such ignorance by applying techniques that won't jeopardize their reputations. For instance, adding high contingency buffers, trying to win the maximum time or cost for the project and minimizing the risk of an overrun. In some cases, the added contingency reserves are absurdly high and go beyond a reasonable buffer for possible delays or higher costs.

Contingency reserves are undoubtedly justified, as we can never guarantee schedule and cost targets. But the problem is that there is rarely a comparison or reference point for projects. Project customers rarely challenge a technology project manager's claims about the delivery time, as they usually lack the technical expertise to understand whether the timeline is justified. But project managers know that project stakeholders challenge cost or schedule targets, even if they have minimal understanding of reasonable targets for a given type of project.

On the other side, project customers know that project managers shoot for the highest budget or longest timelines to make room for possible issues, delays, or unforeseen events. The negotiation game has, in most cases, no proper foundation or justification. The project customer either has no means to appropriately challenge the targets or is entirely unaware that project targets are never written in stone and should not be considered a guarantee.

When projects start to run behind targets, people blame the project managers for not keeping their promises and not doing a good job. Viewing project targets as promises or guarantees is a misconception. It shows a lack of understanding that projects are all about planning and forecasting future events.

As a result, many project managers try to delay commitment for as long as possible. The motivation is clear: if they commit to delivering a project by a specific date, they will be held accountable to that date. Any change may be seen as weakness or incompetence, leading to a loss of confidence in the project manager's capabilities.

Perfectionism

Do you believe perfectionism is a positive trait that everyone should aim for? It can motivate us to achieve excellence and deliver the highest quality in our work. However, so-called perfectionists are often overly critical of themselves and others. This can lead to negative results with anxiety, low self-esteem, high stress and panic. It's the complete opposite effect of what a perfectionist aims for.

The danger in perfectionism is that it can harm performance and is often mistaken for excellence.

Given that project management is about forecasting future events, the constant presence of uncertainty means imperfection is implicit.

PART FOUR

> *Project management excellence does not guarantee success.*

Project management excellence should be about making full and intelligent use of tools, techniques, and methods to forecast and predict project events as best as possible. The goal is to ensure that a project is properly controlled by early identification of potential risks or issues that could impact the planned journey of a project. In addition, it acknowledges the possibility of unforeseen adversity and defines procedures on how to respond so the project is not a wasted effort.

Contrary to what perfectionism implies, project management excellence does not guarantee success. Rather, our efforts to bring a project to a successful conclusion are based on best existing knowledge.

If perfection means always delivering on defined targets, then being a perfectionist in the project management world is a paradox. If a department, organization or project manager has a track record of delivering on initially defined targets, then those projects were practically free of risk, indicating a low or zero risk appetite. That suggests a lack of progress and innovation.

Perfectionism has no place in our domain, primarily because it usually comes with several behaviors that are incompatible with project management.

There are many flaws and limitations in how people manage and run projects. It's unsurprising as human beings are full of imperfections and strengths. You can read deeper on this topic elsewhere in books and academic literature, and I've included a list of suggested further readings in Appendix A.

In many ways, project managers sabotage themselves by trying to please others and save their reputations. It's an impossible situation that they often make worse. But it is less important to hide limitations and flaws, and more important to be aware of them.

Take action. Use your awareness of your limitations and gaps, and employ data and analytics to fill the gaps. With this important work done, it is time to adjust people's behaviors to remove the barriers that block data and analytics capabilities in project management practices.

Chapter takeaways

- Consistent messages and long-applied mental models, rules and practices can lead to an illusion of knowledge or cognitive rigidity and eventually to wrong decisions. It requires the ability to unlearn as previously working practices could become obsolete.
- Be fully aware of people's cognitive limitations and recognize that we are not naturally good at typical project management activities like forecasting or predicting.
- Bringing data and analytics into the project management space requires a culture of transparency and authenticity that allows failure and doesn't encourage people to hide the truth.

PART FOUR

CHAPTER ELEVEN

Removing Barriers

Data and analytics can undoubtedly provide capabilities that extend and complement traditional capabilities in projects. But unlike other project management tools, it is not just something to be installed like software. You can't connect the data pipes, read the manual and get started on data-informed project delivery practices. If you do it this way, practically nothing will change.

Of course, you could operate the same as before and include data and analytics with some nicely designed dashboards and call yourself a data-driven organization. If your goal is to use data to back up what you already know, then you have arrived at your destination. Congratulations!

Stanford professors Robert Sutton and Jeffrey Pfeffer noted in their book *Hard Facts, Dangerous Half-Truths, and Total Nonsense*, "Leaders need to make a fundamental decision: Do they want to be told they are always right, or do they want to lead organizations that perform well?"[1]

If you opted for the latter, read on. This chapter looks at what needs to get out of the way for data and analytics to unfold their value.

In the project management space, that means adopting a new mindset, behaviors and habits, and letting go of old practices that may have become second nature.

....

Enhancing the ability to deal with uncertainty

The important part is that project management practice is about using any available means to enhance and evolve the abilities of project teams to deal with uncertainty and complexity.

People often say that complexity is growing, but I argue that it is changing rather than increasing. Complexity is mainly driven by how many dependencies need to be handled. The number has not increased, there is simply less time to handle them. This leads to faster changing messages and demands, resulting in a need for greater responsiveness, awareness of the unexpected, and improved capabilities to deal with the pace. If you are not keeping up, you become weak, and everything feels like a tremendous burden.

It's like playing soccer. In a professional team, you constantly train and practice with the team, or you get out of shape and fail to win matches. But it's not only about practicing; you also have to keep an eye on methods and tactics. No modern team plays in a defensive formation with a libero (sweeper) as the last defensive player before the goalie. Nowadays, a 4-3-3 formation that uses four defenders behind a midfield line of three is far more common. Soccer evolved; it became faster, more offensive, and more dynamic.

Keeping up with development in environments is critical. It requires an openness to change, experimenting, and exploring new ways of operating. We must constantly train our novelty and innovation muscles to stay competitive.

Overcoming novelty aversion

But novelty often represents a problem, even in projects. That feels like a paradox because projects are supposed to deliver change, and you would reasonably expect project management professionals to be comfortable with novelty.

Some project management tools were introduced almost a century ago, such as the Gantt chart, Pert and Critical Path. While many of those techniques remain highly valuable, their age indicates traditionalism and pushback against new and innovative methods, which may question the validity of traditional tools.

We saw widespread novelty aversion with the introduction of agile methods. The Agile Manifesto was published more than twenty years ago, in 2001. It quickly gained popularity, but many organizations initially rejected it and preferred to rely on traditional methods, even when projects were frequently in trouble due to their lack of flexibility.

We expect the usual and are irritated if we get something else, even if the usual does not seem to be working anymore. Humans have a strong preference for familiarity over variety.[2] When project management techniques and practices go back to the 1950s, they are hard to change or replace.

Today, though, we don't have the luxury of waiting until a method is established before adopting it. By then, it might already be outdated. If

PART FOUR

organizations wait too long to become data-driven, their competitors will be far ahead of them.

....

From a fixed to a growth mindset

Rapid changes ultimately require an entirely new mindset, and we must let go of old and traditional thinking.

Making the most of data analytics requires exploration, creativity and experimentation, which implies taking on challenges with the risk of failure. With a fixed mindset, people prefer to play safe, take the familiar path and play by the rules — even if that doesn't deliver value for the project client.

Regardless of any transition to data-informed practices, project managers should approach with a growth mindset, explore the unknown, be curious about new ways, and seek opportunities. But most don't or are blocked by an unsupportive environment built around success and failure, and reward and punishment. The downside is that people get discouraged over challenging tasks and seek shortcuts instead.

Change requires persistence.

Yet, taking on new challenges and a new path by introducing data analytics may lead to initial disappointment as it probably won't provide the answers you hoped for. That's frustrating, but it's precisely what should happen. Change requires persistence.

It's like learning to walk. Eventually, falling over pays off. We just need to get started.

In many ways, current practices and behaviors limit the effectiveness of our work. This is mainly due to a well-developed fixed mindset. Here are two examples.

The triple constraint

Project management taught us the triple constraint of scope, time and budget. The project manager's role is to keep control by balancing these three constraints most effectively. While this formula is valid, it emphasizes an either/or mentality. "If you want all this, we cannot do all that."[3] It creates a fixed mindset that blocks thinking that would otherwise foster innovation, improvement, and evolution in the project management practice.

When stakeholders seem to demand too much (for example, too much scope for a given timeline or budget), then instead of responding with the triple constraint formula, we must apply out-of-the-box thinking. Challenge your fixed mindset and attempt to deliver the full scope on time and within budget.[4]

While there are obvious limitations, it reframes the triple constraints and turns them into thinking, imagining and experimenting, which are important elements of innovation and evolution. It's like taking off handcuffs you had gotten used to, having forgotten how they limited you.

Project management practice is often impeded by a fixed mindset that follows an approach of "I'm right and you're wrong". This leads to

PART FOUR

political battles that provide no value to projects or the evolution of project management practices.

The goal is to establish a data-informed practice that relies on adaptability, learning, openness to new and frequently changing knowledge, and collective intelligence. Project professionals and executives must adopt a growth mindset that acknowledges that they could be wrong and others may know better.

Replace "I am right and you're wrong" with "I have a valuable point of view, but I may be missing something". This sounds easy, but it isn't, as corporate titles and egos get in the way. "Who are you telling me I am wrong?" This new kid on the block (analytics) will produce insights that may challenge some people's opinions.

The psychologist Carol Dweck suggested the terms *fixed* and *growth mindset* to explain that people's views and beliefs determine the development of their qualities and intelligence.[5] With a fixed mindset, we take our capability as given and constantly look for proof and confirmation. A growth mindset is based on learning from mistakes, gaining experience outside our comfort zone, practicing the new and unknown, and questioning established practices and habits.

Project management uses a lot of heuristics and mental models that haven't changed in decades. That doesn't mean we should abandon those that are still applicable and useful, but we must keep exploring and validating practices.

From fear to purpose

All project management professionals need to adopt the practices of learning, unlearning and relearning. That inevitably means letting go of the fear of failure. Many organizations follow a strategy of not being first-movers in areas such as implementing new standard software or rolling out a new version of an off-the-shelf product. This is all about risk mitigation, as a new version could have a lot of bugs. It's like when Microsoft comes out with a new version of their Windows operating system. Many people want to delay installing it as they fear the initial version might be buggy.

Ok, fair enough. I wouldn't want to be a first adopter here, either. But, over time, such behaviors became habitual.

A data-informed and evidence-based project delivery practice requires an exploratory and creative mindset from all participants and stakeholders to evolve and prosper. We need first movers and people who are open to failure. It also means letting go of fears about making wrong decisions, as these may lead to overanalyzing by looking at too much data.

Fear of failure delays decision-making. Often decisions need to be made quickly to keep momentum. Don't base everything on data. Instead, combine the best available

> *Fear of failure delays decision-making.*

data with experience. It is tempting to see data as the ultimate and only evidence on which to make bullet-proof decisions. That thinking will result in no decision because you will be driven by the fear of missing existing information. You will never have enough information to eliminate your fears. Making use of data and analytics should not invalidate experience and intuition.

PART FOUR

Be irrational in your decisions

In this context, we must be more open and mindful of the irrationality of decisions. After all, irrationality is based on subjective filters. A decision-maker isn't making an irrational decision when applying their best knowledge, experience and expertise. But the decision may appear so to others who lack a full view of the criteria, motivations, supporting data and beliefs.

When adding the insights derived from data for data-informed decision-making, the resulting conclusions could appear irrational, but they are not. Yet we label the decisions as poor, having run them through our personal, biased filters. Watch for that and learn to let go of unhelpful preconceptions. Assume there is no such thing as irrationality.

Instead of judging, ask questions about the criteria used, and understand the factors that contributed to the decision. In other words, learn to be irrational based on your personal standards and criteria.

....

Drive collaboration

PART FOUR

Collective intelligence implies that collaboration maximizes available intelligence. This starts with sharing data and knowledge with other teams and departments, which seems obvious but is rarely done effectively.

Collaboration can include other organizations exchanging ideas, insights and practices. A good example is a blockchain consortium led by startup R3 CEV, with forty-two banks participating.[6] The goal is to partner up for the standardized use of distributed ledger technology, including exchanging client onboarding information for faster onboarding procedures by participating banks. That helps the bank to keep costs low, and the customer gets faster service.

In project management, many pray for collaboration but (especially in today's gig economy) project professionals are often more focused on the success of their current project. At best, they share learning and information within their department, even though other projects certainly could benefit from project learning and best practices.

Become disciplined

Employing data and analytics in projects requires diligence and discipline by project management staff towards improved performance. It's like preparing dinner for family and friends; you

Employing data and analytics in projects requires diligence and discipline.

may create a perfect dish but leave a mess in the kitchen. At some point, the kitchen needs to be cleaned, used dishes washed, leftovers placed in the refrigerator, and so on. Restaurants approach this process diligently and with discipline; otherwise, they become messy, filthy, risky and, eventually, close down.

In the project management space, the table orders come in so frequently that, over time, diligence and discipline are forgotten and things become an inefficient mess. If we skip returning leftovers to the fridge, they rot away and are unusable. We have to throw them away and make new ones. Uncleaned dishes become unusable and have to be replaced. Get the picture?

PART FOUR

PART FOUR

That is more or less how many project management shops operate, primarily because of growing pressures to work faster. And there is less and less time to clean up our mess after a project is delivered. Lessons Learned sessions are rarely done (at least not productively), and project artifacts are not properly stored or shared.

Recycle the data

Being careless with project data increases the risk of failure as projects struggle to find relevant information. Data needs to be stored in a structurally consistent way to be accessible for insights and learning. It needs to be recycled to build a circular project economy. While this should be embedded in internal rules and policies, we shouldn't have to enforce it as the project managers themselves will benefit from it. In the end, this data is fuel for analytics and helps projects to perform better.

It needs to become second nature.

Be authentic and transparent

One of the most important elements of a data-informed project management practice is ensuring a culture of transparency, truth, authenticity and accountability. As we discussed in Chapter Eight, evidence-driven projects rely heavily on a culture of candor.

Think about it. The key elements of project data are the artifacts produced by project leaders and teams. Project plans, schedules, and so forth should provide an overview of what is going on in a project. How would that work if project people aren't truthful, transparent, accountable and authentic?

Data is what we make of it. Garbage in, garbage out.

The need for project resilience

While many project organizations are quick to request advanced statistics and data analytics to improve project performance and reduce failures, exhaust existing knowledge first. Given the lack of cross-team collaboration in many organizations, there is certainly potential to stretch this knowledge to build effective project resilience.

> *Exhaust existing knowledge first.*

In an age where disruptions and frequent (and often unforeseen) changes are becoming the norm, it is important to create resilience so projects are resistant while remaining on track toward the goals.

Resilience is usually seen as some sort of defense mechanism with the ability to bounce back from adversity. For example, a project team member gets sick and is off work for several months. This can, of course, happen in any project. Hopefully, the project manager will have taken precautionary measures and distributed project knowledge, activities and skills so another team member can take over the tasks. That ensures the project can still operate despite the temporary loss. Resilience is in place if a project bounces back when a negative event hits. It's like a boxing fight where you are hit hard, stumble and maybe even fall, but you get up and go on. The hit makes you pause and rethink, but you don't lose the fight.

In today's environment, that definition of resilience needs to be adjusted. Merely bouncing back is no longer possible because projects deal with risks that turn into issues and, increasingly, with disruption and truly game-changing events. Remember how the pandemic caught many organizations and projects by surprise? Many organizations

PART FOUR

were resilient enough to get through and proceed. But many did not bounce back because there was nothing to bounce back to. The old normal was gone.

Organizations adapted to a new normal, with staff working from home, ensuring proper IT infrastructure was in place to manage the increased online load, etc. Nobody knew how long the new normal would last, and, eventually, it permanently changed our whole way of working, with hybrid work becoming the status quo in many organizations.

Conditions can change rapidly, and in many cases, projects need to be prepared to replan and switch directions altogether without getting paralyzed or stuck by sudden changes. Not reacting or adapting fast enough could mean a project fails.

Adaptability is key, but being prepared and informed appropriately and in good time has become a critical element of project resilience. The more information and knowledge we have about a project, the affected business environments, external and internal factors, and practically a 360-degree view of the project, the more we can adapt quickly to new conditions.[7]

PART FOUR

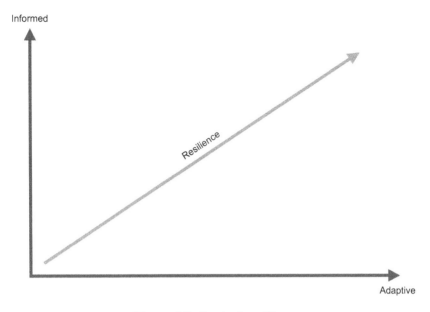

Informed

Resilience

Adaptive

Figure 29: Project resilience

As figure 29 shows, both adaptive and informed mindsets support themselves because the more aware and adept you become, the more information you produce by learning, sharing and experiencing. The more informed you are, the more you can exercise an adaptive capacity.

This means that being informed doesn't start with employing data analytics or any advanced data technology. It begins with capturing and valuing information and knowledge gained through experience, sharing it with other teams or departments, standardizing lessons learned,

Being informed doesn't start with employing data analytics.

PART FOUR

and using knowledge management systems, project management information systems (PMIS) and best practices.

Additional relevant data and insights, including data analytics, will further improve project resilience, but that shouldn't mean traditional ways of being informed don't apply. Data and analytics do not replace existing knowledge; they complement it with additional insights. Hence, before applying data-informed practices, exhaust any other means that can lift project knowledge and resilience.

That includes having governance that supports information and knowledge exchange. Set up cross-functional teams to ensure that previously separate teams (e.g., business users, change management teams, and IT teams) collaborate closely and better understand each other's challenges, problems, concerns and ideas.

Business users often are far away from technology teams. They don't understand why implementation is so difficult, while IT teams often don't know what drives users' demands. Bringing people from different functions closer helps eliminate misunderstandings and provides opportunities to foreshadow problems.

That is just one example of how you can lift the level of informedness in your project and project management practice. Alongside the necessary adaptive capacity, this helps establish resilience that may not withstand hurricanes but will certainly weather some heavy storms.

Some managers think that applying agile methods in their projects protects them from being overrun by disruption and adversity, but this approach is no longer good enough.

The first step is to know where you stand, how prepared your project management practice is, and what the gaps are.

Figure 30 illustrates the different states of survival and the action needed to move to a resilient state and prepare to introduce data-informed practices. Let's unpack each quadrant.

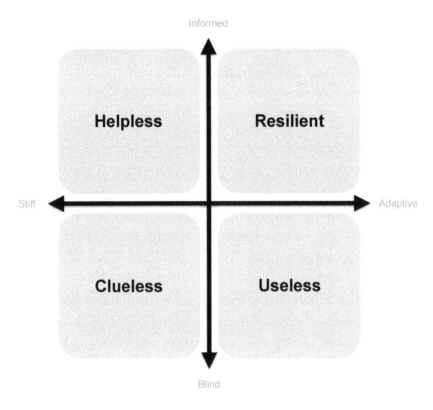

Figure 30: Getting out of survival mode

Clueless

Project teams operate with blinders if they are unaware of their environment and related changes and trends. When disruptive and unplanned events hit, they may not comprehend the events or have an appropriate and informed response. Adapting to the changes may be their only option.

It's like a journalist who is ill-informed and inflexible when writing for a particular magazine. The interests of a magazine audience change over time, but the journalist may be unaware of such trends because there is no such analysis of reader behaviors and interests. The magazine's rules and policy may mandate sticking with the usual way of writing. Eventually, people abandon the magazine because it no longer addresses their interests.

Helpless

While project teams rely on information to identify trends and foresee potential change and disruption, such information is useless unless acted upon. That means project professionals must adapt quickly and redirect their efforts based on information received and a likely new reality. Otherwise, they are helpless and unable to use the information and apply derived knowledge.

Imagine that the journalist receives new information that would make a big headline, but is reluctant (or not allowed) to drop their current article and work on the new story. That's being informed without adaptability.

Useless

Reacting and adapting quickly requires sufficient information on the best response to emerging trends, adversity and changing conditions, to ensure that a project still delivers value.

The journalist can cope with changing conditions, news and trends, but articles are useless unless the audience wants to read them.

Teams must understand the nature and impact of change, and how it can transform the value proposition of the project. Without that information, they will likely try to return to the original state and plan, which may now be obsolete. Teams steer their efforts towards a new reality with a mindset of learning and constantly learning about trends.

Becoming resilient

Project teams that are not informed and adaptive are crippled and unable to respond appropriately to disruption and unplanned events.

Resilience ensures today's dynamics do not overrun them. Disruption, unplanned change and failures are inevitable. Learning from these builds a mindset that looks for new opportunities. In this sense, it is useful to see resilience as a way to make your project organization future-ready, not a defense mechanism.[8]

> *See resilience as a way to make your project organization future-ready.*

....

Know your project

The more knowledge you have about potential risks and threats, the better. Proper assessment and investigation help you understand the project from all angles and prepare for possible scenarios.

As mentioned earlier, I used to work in the compliance domain within large international banks, specifically in anti-financial crime and anti-money laundering. I was responsible for applications for client screening processes. Let me explain. When someone opens a bank account or relationship, a background screening process determines if the bank is allowed and wants to do business with that person. This process is called *Know Your Customer* (KYC) and includes diligent processes to verify the identity and any potential risks attached to the person and a possible business relationship. Basically, it asks, "Is there a threat?"

As part of a KYC process, analysts conduct in-depth research on account documents, verifying the potential existence of any restrictions or negative activities that could impact the account opening. In addition, the KYC analyst reviews policies, compliance and market trends. The customer may have a distant connection or relationship with someone who would represent a risk. All this information completes the picture of a customer and allows the bank to make an informed decision about opening the account.

These analysts must be highly skilled in decision-making, time management and research, and have an eye for risks and threats.[9] Depending on the type of customer, a process of enhanced due diligence (EDD) may apply. It requires analysis of additional information to provide a deeper understanding of customer activity to mitigate associated risks. In many ways, the analyst role holds traits you would expect to see in a project manager.

It's useful to imagine acting like a KYC analyst. Becoming a KYP analyst means you will Know Your Project inside out with enhanced due diligence, to work out any risks or threats and build potential scenarios. This must include a sound analysis of current trends and developments.

PART FOUR

All this builds a resilience muscle that is strengthened over time with diligence. Eventually, it replaces reactivity with much needed proactivity. You move from defense to offense in your project management practice.

Chapter takeaways

- Project management is often driven based on a fixed mindset, with a rigid focus on long-established rules and guidelines, instead of embracing a growth mindset where people release the fear of wrong decisions.

- While many project organizations are quick to request advanced statistics and data analytics to improve project performance and reduce failures, existing knowledge should first be exhausted.

- See resilience as a way to make your project organization future-ready, not as a defense mechanism.

PART FOUR

CHAPTER TWELVE

Enabling Evidence-based Practices

In the last chapter, we looked at what needs to get out of the way to transition to data-informed and evidence-based practices. In terms of people's behaviors and resulting culture, that's half the battle.

The next step is to enable such practices and make them work. You own a powerful engine called data analytics, and now you must prepare the body of your car to make it fit. You are doing the groundwork for this engine to unleash its power.

This chapter looks at the traits and characteristics we need to adopt to follow a data-informed approach and not fall back into patterns where intuition and human reasoning dominate.

....

Upskill project leaders

Upskilling is more than reading a manual, watching some videos, and leaving the rest to practice. Of course, practice is the key, but it isn't as simple as that.

People often see emerging technologies and concepts like AI and machine learning as tools that need plugging in to provide immediate value. But before using the tools, teams must understand how analytics works, how data works, and how we generate insights. And how people can and should work in such a setup.

The key element of upskilling is changing mindsets and habits and opening up to new ways of working. Unlike conventional project tools, analytics relies on people's behaviors, input and engagement. It is not just software that you roll out, then allow people to decide whether to use it. Analytics is not an add-on to current practices. We cannot mandate its use, and it does not replace subject matter knowledge or free us from thinking.

Data and analytics is often regarded as a way of systemizing project management processes. And while artificial intelligence, machine learning and robotics will eventually help automate trivial decisions, the wrong approach would be to get into analytics expecting to offload your work to a machine so you can work on other stuff.

The goal is to become more accurate in project planning, risk management and decision-making. Adding data and analytics raises the bar for knowledge and evidence. And this, in turn, means investing far more effort into thinking, questioning, challenging, sense-making, and maintenance and aggregation of knowledge.

Technology is ineffective without the right skill set and tools.

Only this understanding and mindset will enable value from analytics tools, as wrong expectations and misconceptions will be counterproductive and even harm performance. Technology is ineffective without the right skill set and tools. It's like driving a car before learning how.

It's not an IT thing

That doesn't mean everyone needs to become a data scientist or overly technical. The necessary skills are understanding where data comes from, how it is processed, how it contributes to knowledge and evidence, and how it helps to get to the truth.

Some may think that it is the IT department's responsibility to collect data, curate and process data, and provide insights to business users. But the transition to data-informed practices concerns everyone in an organization, including the CEO.

The value of data teams and data scientists is in processing data to generate new insights to solve business problems and make decisions. This requires deep domain knowledge and an ability to translate business problems into the right questions that narrow the selection of relevant data for analysis to eventually reach relevant answers and insights.

Stephen Few is a well-respected expert and innovator in business intelligence and data visualization. He noted in his book, *The Data Loom,* that the better our knowledge of a particular subject or domain, the better we get at making sense of related data.[1]

Bridge the gap between data and insights

Data and business teams work together to derive genuine value from data and make it actionable.

While data teams work with raw data and maintain and manage data, they rely on subject matter experts and their domain expertise to narrow down required data sets to identify relevant patterns that eventually lead to insights for decision-making. This is illustrated in figure 31.

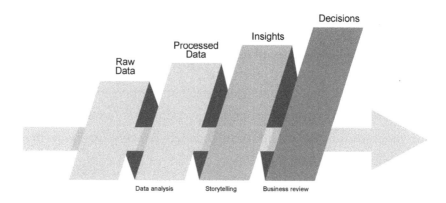

Figure 31: From raw data to decisions

Data storytelling is often underrated, although it is probably the most important element in the lifecycle, from raw data to insights. When sourced, data runs through a technical workflow, where data analysts process raw data and turn it into readable information.

The next step is connecting the dots between the data processing part and the business actions triggered by elaborated insights. Generating insights is crucial and requires data storytelling to communicate actionable takeaways.

While this concept is generally applicable in data-driven environments, it calls for new roles and responsibilities in the project management domain. These might include a data analyst who acts as the middleman, with sufficient understanding of a particular project, its business area, and the challenges, unknowns and risks. They work closely with the

PART FOUR

project team, translating questions related to unknowns into actionable and workable input. With collected, processed and readable data, we identify patterns that feed into a data story and eventual insights for decision-making.

This is a simplified example; the reality would include several iterations of data processing and analysis. But the key is that a layer of translation, commonly referred to as data storytelling, generates insights. Without insights, no actions will be taken, making data storytelling a critical element in this workflow.

Data literacy

These concepts form part of a broader term called data literacy. I mention this here as there is often misunderstanding about who it is relevant for. Data literacy is often seen as simply another term for data science, but that could not be further from the truth.

Jordan Morrow is head of Data and Analytics at the software training company BrainStorm. He is often referred to as the Godfather of data literacy, given his contributions to the data and analytics community. In *Be Data Literate,* he described data literacy as the ability to read data, work with data, analyze data and communicate with data.[2] It's easy to fall into the trap of thinking that IT teams should take care of this. However, given organizations are increasingly data-driven, everyone should be data literate and understand how to act with data.

Data and analytics are supposed to answer business questions that help bring projects to a successful conclusion. We need to learn to ask the right questions and draw the right conclusions. Data literacy means engaging and interacting with data. Morrow indicated three

PART FOUR

traits we should possess to become data literate, labeling them as the three Cs of data literacy.

Curiosity

The best and most impactful insights are the result of curiosity. Curiosity is the motivation and impulse to seek new or additional information. Natural curiosity triggers the ability to ask further critical questions around data that bring us closer to answers that provide value.

Remember that data does not provide insights; it tells you what questions to ask next. That means project data is practically useless unless we are curious enough to interact with it. Keep asking questions to interpret the data you are exposed to. Only the right questions lead to insights.

It's the same with decision-making. Data and statistics need presenting in ways that provide information and trigger deep thinking. We want to develop creative or innovative solutions or the motivation to explore a particular message further. It improves solution finding, management of uncertainties, and the quality of decision-making.

Creativity

Freeing yourself from the constraints of processes and requirements and the need to know everything, means you are more open to taking risks, letting ideas flow, and experimenting with the unknown. Running experiments makes you more likely to find surprising opportunities or answers, because you didn't know or had wrong assumptions. It's like painting with colors instead of using black and white. Mix them and see what new colors you generate.

Experimentation brings surprises, which are a fundamental source of innovation.

> *Experimentation brings surprises.*

Critical thinking

While data should help project professionals be less biased and make more informed decisions, there is a risk of arranging data so we see what we want to see. Data samples may not adequately represent a population, leading to early and often wrong conclusions. We must learn how to disprove data, even if the collected insights seem logical. Making sense of data requires critical thinking skills. Otherwise, we risk falling into the trap of fake news.

We also need to be critical of the insights derived from data and not jump to conclusions based on mere assumptions. Just as analytics can be a sparring partner for human judgment, data and analytics need a sparring partner in the form of human intellect and intuition.

Adopt a statistical mindset for learning and action

A statistical mindset means investing in data sensemaking. Stephen Few noted that such skills are usually underrated due to a misconception around vendor tools that promise self-service analytics and undermine the need for upskilling employees with data-sense-making skills.[3] It speaks to my earlier point that working with data and analytics does not mean you can sit back, push a button, and have project forecasting magically presented to your manager.

Again, critical thinking is essential here. When looking at information and data from projects, a statistical mindset engages critical thinking

PART FOUR

and looks at the world as it is. It triggers our learning from data towards action.

Basic statistics training can remarkably change how project forecasting is done. Using statistical thinking in projects is certainly not new, but it gains importance as data exponentially increases.

The use of data in projects provides an opportunity for an outside view to answer a particular question. Let's say an organization wants to introduce a new enterprise resource planning (ERP) system and is unsure which off-the-shelf software would be most suitable. An inside view would offer a more subjective opinion; for example, an executive or a group of stakeholders often has a clear preference for particular software. But it is advisable to take a more statistical or outside view to make an informed decision. An outside view could include statistics about various ERP systems and their market presence. It might involve client feedback, indicating which systems are most popular, most user-friendly. Ideally, use a mix of inside and outside opinions, combining statistical and personal experience.[4]

Psychologist Daniel Kahneman popularized the concept of inside and outside views, which is also used in reference class forecasting.[5] This method was further developed for the project management domain by Oxford University professor Bent Flyvbjerg, who regards it as the most accurate method for project forecasting.[6] The method was introduced to overcome typically highly biased human judgment by applying an uplift to project estimates based on forecasting discrepancies in similar historical projects.[7]

....

Evidence is a guide to truth

Deriving valuable insights based on historical projects (as with the reference class forecasting method) contributes to project knowledge and leads to more informed project decisions and judgments.

When making a judgment about a particular situation or scenario, we apply knowledge based on collected evidence. It usually starts with an assumption that might be a hunch based on reasonable suspicion. When forecasting a project, we work with estimates and input from the project team, which means experience and, to some extent, intuition. Given the collective input, this approach is usually considered rational. But it remains an assumption as it lacks proof and has no real basis for informed and sound decision-making.

We want to get to a 'Prove it' culture.

Before we look into the meaning of evidence, let's clarify what an assumption is.

An assumption is an unwarrantable claim that you believe is true but is not (yet) backed up with information and evidence. It is essentially a hypothesis based on insufficient reasoning. An assumption is largely insufficient because it is often subjective, biased and based on conclusions that are not proven universally valid.

Consequently, we usually look for facts and information that guide us toward sound judgment. The validity of the judgment depends on how well those facts support the claims.

211

We want to get to a 'Prove it' culture based on scientific reasoning, which involves a process of claim, evidence and reasoning:

> Claim: What do you know?
>
> Evidence: How do you know that?
>
> Reasoning: How does your evidence support your claim?

Hence, coming up with evidence for a claim or assumption gives us a direction to better understand the claim, but it may not be sufficient to stand as genuine evidence.

What happens if it doesn't support the claim and gives a different direction?

I recently went shopping for sports shoes for running. At the store, I looked up the model and size I wanted. The store was arranged so different sizes weren't visible, so I assumed a shoe was a size 9½ just by looking at it. To be certain, I checked the inside label for evidence to support my assumption. But the label showed a size 10½.

It's an experience many of us have had when buying shoes and clothing. If the label had shown the expected size, I could have taken it as sufficient evidence to go ahead and buy the shoes.

But if you are like me, you would need more evidence to satisfy your belief. I needed evidence for the evidence. So I tried on the shoe, and it turned out to be too large, so I had to look for one with a label of 9½. Effectively, evidence guided me to make an informed judgment.

On another shoe-buying occasion, I faced the same situation; only it turned out that size 10½ was the right fit. Apparently there's a difference between shoe manufacturers. Where was the evidence?

PART FOUR

Initially, it was the shoe label, then trying on the shoe. The proper term for this is higher-order evidence which provides some extended assurance about the validity of the first-order evidence. It is effectively testing the reliability of the evidence. First-order evidence can turn out to be invalid because it may have been misinterpreted or is not trustworthy.[8,9]

It's like a weather report. If the weather data indicates it will be sunny tomorrow, then we have first-order evidence and a resulting expectation of fine weather. But if higher-order evidence shows that the weather report is wrong

> *Belief is essential to establish valid evidence.*

in eighty percent of cases, it would invalidate our belief in the initial evidence. Belief is essential to establish valid evidence. This is illustrated in figure 32.[10]

The Collins Online Dictionary defines evidence as "anything that you see, experience, read, or are told that causes you to believe that something is true or has happened".[11] The emphasis here is on belief.

To have fully justified belief leading to truth, we need both belief in our claims and evidence to support them.

PART FOUR

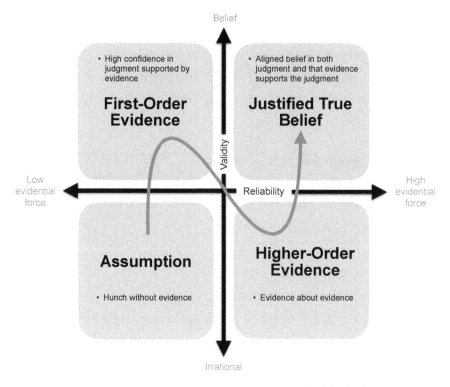

Figure 32: From assumption to justified belief

We often see collected data as evidence for our claims. This is dangerous because evidence holds, or should hold, more than just data. As my shoe shopping example illustrates, a message derived from data (the size label) could be proven wrong within a given context.

By seeking evidence and becoming truly evidence-based in our decision-making, we generate interactions between different sources of knowledge, be they data, experience, intuition, or anything considered a relevant source of knowledge that improves the quality of our decisions. And that interaction raises questions that guide us toward the truth.

In *Hard Facts, Dangerous Half-Truths, and Total Nonsense*, Jeffrey Pfeffer and Robert Sutton explain that evidence-based practices require a different mindset, mainly an openness and willingness to take

> *Seeking truth means accepting that you could be wrong.*

facts seriously instead of insisting on one's claim and beliefs.[12] There is no point in gathering facts and evidence if they have no power to influence your beliefs. Seeking truth means accepting that you could be wrong.

Let's return to our project forecast based on rational decision-making. We can seek evidence by reviewing historical projects with similar characteristics and conditions, and making a comparison. But we know that no project is like another. Yet, there are similarities, and such comparisons could serve as first-order evidence. Remember, though, that an outside view should be mixed with an inside view based on people's experience and intuition. The initial assumption was weak in terms of belief, the first-order evidence guided us to come up with a first evidenced estimate, and the higher-order evidence made sense of it in combination with experience. The result is a justified true belief.

Here's an example of the different steps to a project forecast.

1. We want to forecast a software development project and take the traditional approach to estimate tasks, add contingency reserve, and so on, and come up with a timeline. The project duration is estimated to be eight months up to the point of delivery.

2. We are seeking evidence and collecting data from historical projects for a comparison in terms of timelines. For example,

PART FOUR

let's use reference class forecasting. The accumulated evidence indicates that the estimate of eight months is way too optimistic. A recommended uplift would be six months for a total duration of fourteen months.

3. When they mix the outside view from step two with an inside view (insights from experience and intuition), the project team realizes that twelve months will be unacceptable to the client. Based on further analysis of the different tasks and dependencies, they understand that adding two additional developers to the team will reduce the project duration to ten months. However, on reviewing past referenced projects, the previous teams had usually worked together already for a while. The current project comprises a completely new team, with new hires from outside the organization. The project manager believes this will slow down the initial progress as team-building activities will be required. He estimates two months to be sufficient for team-forming activities, so the final timeline is twelve months.

Evidence guides the estimation process in this case, but it is not limited to data and analytics. It serves as a guide but should not be the sole driver of the verdict. Knowledge — the mix of data and analytics, experience and intuition — drives evidence.

In this particular forecasting example (as with most scenarios in the project management world), there is additional higher-order evidence in the form of actual project duration. That turns into genuine fact and forms a reference for future projects.

Enhance your critical thinking

The appropriate knowledge mix that drives evidence requires good critical thinking skills. Remember my earlier point about acting like Columbo, the TV inspector from the 1970s? Our natural tendency is to find ways to make things easier. Humans like to use heuristics that model answers based on familiar situations. This often leads to simplification, thus avoiding asking and answering the right questions.

It's not helpful to assume that data and analytics will make the project manager's life easier. This sounds like automation or dumping some numbers into a calculator to spit out a result. The difference we expect is not the amount of work but the effectiveness of our work.

> *The difference we expect is not the amount of work but the effectiveness of our work.*

Learn to be wrong

We often mentally calculate something simple, such as summing simple figures, then use a calculator to validate whatever we have (usually confidently) worked out. The confirmation makes us feel more convinced, even if it is simple math, and there is no doubt that the calculator would get the same result. So why do we do it? And more importantly, what would we do if we didn't get the confirmation and the calculator proved us wrong?

A critical analytical mindset means letting data question your judgments, no matter how obvious and clear your solution seems to be. We've already seen that humans too often fall for cognitive traps they don't recognize. Data and analytics can validate our views, and

PART FOUR

Never immediately believe insights from data.

the reference class forecasting method is a good example.

For this to work, project professionals must be open to being wrong and adopt critical thinking skills to question data and its messages. The game of analytics is mainly about getting various insights and using them to get closer to the truth. While people can be proven wrong by the insights from analytics, such confrontation of different views should trigger questions. A debate, if you will.

Never immediately believe insights from data. How often have you heard or read something and said, "No way!" or "That cannot be true". We question messages and seek evidence that could prove something we didn't expect or don't want to see. That is where a change in thinking happens. We need to learn to be wrong.

It sounds easy, but, in practice, it often isn't.

On the other hand, asking questions about what seems to be fact and evidence but hasn't convinced us may uncover flaws in data or sense-making from insights and patterns in data. It is this interaction and questioning that brings us closer to the truth.

Experimentation generates surprises

The side effect of consciously realizing that it's impossible to know everything, is that we are more open to taking risks, letting ideas flow, and experimenting more with the unknown. And by running experiments, we are more likely to find opportunities or answers

PART FOUR

that surprise us because we didn't know it before or had wrong assumptions.

The concept of experimentation was made popular in books such as *The Lean Startup* by Eric Ries[13] and by the design company IDEO[14] whose approach to innovation and product prototyping is through design thinking and experimentation.

Experimentation became popular with companies like Airbnb and Spotify because it generates new knowledge fast. The more you experiment, the more you know about what works and what doesn't. Innovation is based on experimentation. That means it can help resolve some of the biggest unknowns, including in the project management space.

You can see different flavors of it within the various agile methods. Something doesn't seem to work as expected, and people come up with hybrid models such as Scrumban. Those are ideas turned into knowledge.

In getting to data-informed practices, you will have no choice but to experiment and be genuinely curious about the results. Data alone is not knowledge. It needs investigating to test hypotheses in various iterations, and eventually become information and knowledge. This is valid for data analysts and IT staff, and it applies to everyone in contact with data in any way.

PART FOUR

....

Enable data and analytics

It's easy to associate this with leveraging data technology, wrangling data, aligning data quality and setting up new processes. While those changes are part of a transition to data-informed practices, people are the key to success. Changing their behaviors, established habits and mindsets, and forming a new project culture enable data to contribute to expanded knowledge.

We must also remove any possible roadblocks for new insights to make an impact.

It is the expansion of an existing collective intelligence based on groups of people acting coherently. They collaborate and aggregate their knowledge to build collective intelligence. Extending the collective with data analytics is like adding a new ingredient that affects the taste and flavor of the whole dish.

Diversity of opinions enables collective intelligence.

Think about making soup. A new ingredient makes it richer and tastier, but you must stir the soup to unlock the flavor. The ingredients in your project soup are knowledge and insights from human experience, expertise and intuition, and from data and analytics. Combining those insights forms enhanced knowledge and offers greater insights based on collective intelligence. Those different insights need to be synthesized; otherwise, we create knowledge silos.[15]

PART FOUR

Build collective intelligence

Projects rely on collective effort. They are rarely based on the skills and knowledge of one person. A combined effort means there is combined knowledge and collective intelligence at work. James Surowiecki wrote about this in *The Wisdom of Crowds*, highlighting that aggregated information and knowledge from groups outsmart the knowledge of a single individual.[16] The diversity of opinions and expertise that a collective provides is the key to higher accuracy and quality of decisions, leading eventually to higher chances of project success.

While this seems obvious, examples of collective intelligence have left little room for different opinions and diversity. The financial crisis of 2007 serves as a negative example due to a lack of diversity in market opinion that caused an overly optimistic outlook and ignored risks related to the housing market.[17]

Diversity of opinions enables collective intelligence.

Enable diversity

Project leaders often hire team members for cultural fit and run several rounds with HR to understand if someone aligns with organizational values and whether their profile and character will improve team performance.

Yet what traits and characteristics (beyond the hard skills) would promise a lift in team performance?

Often, people are seen as a cultural fit if they have a similar profile to others on the team and share the same work preferences and behaviors. Hiring managers seem to believe these result in harmony among team

PART FOUR

221

members and higher productivity as skill sets complement each other and are used optimally.

But diversity among people and views is key to performance, progress and effectiveness. You need a mix of optimists, pessimists, troublemakers, leaders and followers. Hiring for cultural fit can result in a lack of diversity. People may not challenge each other with different thoughts, ideas, or perspectives.

Many organizations promote diversity and inclusion in their workforce, but they associate diversity primarily with race, skin color, religion, gender, etc. That does not necessarily mean diversity of opinions, ideas and perspectives. Many surveys and statistics focus on gender or ethnic diversity, which research confirms improves the financial performance of firms.[18] Yet, we should not hire simply for the right ratios of gender or ethnicity. It's more important that they increase overall performance.

Diversity removes barriers to progress.

Diversity in a team should primarily mean that people do not align on their views, habits and practices but respect each other's views. Diversity removes barriers that often exist in conformity with norms and standards. But standards are never the end of knowledge. Rather, they are established practices that require further development and evolution not to become obsolete.

For example, you do not want a project team full of agilists who all align on a delivery methodology. You want controversy where people may argue that another methodology could be more suitable than Agile on a certain project.

For projects in general, you don't want a bunch of yay-sayers who keep running through routine procedures, as this will inevitably end in failure. I believe that if there is too much harmony in the team and the project appears to go down the happy path, then something is deeply wrong, and I would be worried. But you may struggle to pinpoint the precise issue. You need diversity in the team, including troublemakers and pessimists, because they always find the hair in the soup. For projects to perform well and not be derailed by unforeseen issues, project managers need to know about that hair in the soup as it could cause significant turbulence.

If we want data-informed practices to work in project management, we do not want a team of analytics-centered data radicals who believe that data is a single source of truth. Just as biased behaviors and irrational judgments need challenging, we must also question the insights that data and analytics hold.

How does diversity result in better performance? By triggering debates, discussion, questioning, rethinking, reframing, and eventually getting teams closer to truth and accuracy. Diversity removes barriers to progress.

Environments that are not diverse stand still and stagnate, operating continuously with the same old practices and ignoring the need for evolution. However, building a diverse workforce is not enough to shake things up because even groups of diverse people are naturally limited.

Don't become a data activist

We should partner with data but not become data activists. As organizations embark on becoming data-driven and triggering

PART FOUR

223

initiatives in the project management domain, there is a risk of relying too much on data and disregarding other sources of knowledge, such as experience, intuition and gut feeling.

> *Data is only one source of knowledge.*

Data is only one source of knowledge. It is insufficient alone, as data-derived insights cannot answer every question. Nor can human intuition and experience, so it takes a combination to provide balance and hybrid intelligence.

Align decision-maker types

Risk has various faces and depends on the manager whose decision-making style relates to their background, preferences, beliefs, and confidence level. All managers and decision-makers must embrace data and share a common understanding of the use of data and analytics, to establish data-informed decision-making.

Accordingly, it is important to identify the different decision-making types in an organization and apply relevant measures to align them, as suggested by Simone Gressel, David J. Pauleen, and Nazim Taskin in their book *Management Decision-Making, Big Data and Analytics*.[19] Let's look more closely at the elements shown in figure 33.

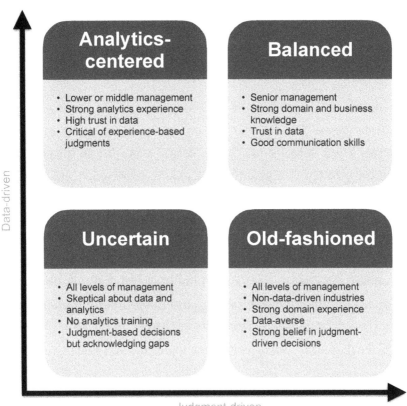

Figure 33: Decision-maker types (adapted)[20]

Analytics-centered

Younger generations are often more scientifically driven, with extensive experience with analytics and trust in data. While very data-savvy, they tend to place less sway on contextual or domain knowledge and rely heavily on data. You will identify them in decision-making meetings or steering committees as they usually open with, "The data says that...."

PART FOUR

225

Such statements show the imbalance between analytics and human insights from experience and expertise. They are also an attempt to transfer the responsibility for a decision to the underlying data. Essentially, they are saying, "It wasn't me. The data is to blame."

The messages gleaned from data depend on the quality of the questions we ask. We can't blame data for a wrong decision. Instead, it indicates a lack of focus on experience and expertise. In the end, data has nothing to say. Our assumptions, claims, experience and intuition give data a voice.

One solution to being too data-driven is exposing people to the details and day-to-day activities of the business. Analytics-centered people are usually too deep in data and technology and don't see the whole from a business point of view. Being closer to business functions helps them see how data informs people's decisions. In the end, data does not make decisions; business leaders, managers and executives do.

Old-fashioned

Old-fashioned often infers an older generation, who follow traditional experience-based approaches and perhaps reject data altogether. They usually work for traditional and non-data-driven organizations. You can identify them when they refer to their years of experience, indicating that they have nothing to learn anymore and that they supersede anyone with less experience and anything novel. Have you heard this somewhere? "I have thirty years of experience. Who are you to tell me that I am wrong?"

They have a strong aversion to data which (besides formal data and analytics training) requires an upfront agreement and buy-in regarding what data is selected and how it will be used in the decision-making process. When using data in decisions, show it in a highly understandable format. A few bar charts (or worse, an Excel table) will not encourage them to be more open to data. Visuals that use data tell a story with good visualization. I highly recommend you read Stephen Few's books *Show Me The Numbers* and *Now You See It*.[21,22]

Uncertain

This group is highly skeptical about the value of data and analytics. Yet they also believe human intuition and experience are insufficient. The outcome could be decision paralysis because they overthink, seeking more and more information. But there is never just the right amount of information.[23] If they lack data skills, they may reject data unless it confirms their opinions, claims, or assumptions.

Demonstrating and explaining how to understand how data and analytics relate to the performance of projects (i.e., how data effectively informs project decisions) can help to build trust in a data-informed practice.[24]

Balanced

A balanced decision-making approach must be the goal of a data-informed project management practice. This type of decision-maker has an excellent understanding of data analytics concepts. They appreciate the value of data in the process and equally apply contextual and domain knowledge, experience and intuition. They trust and explore both sources of knowledge and carefully make decisions.

PART FOUR

Chapter takeaways

- Getting to data-informed practices is not only for IT departments; it affects everyone in an organization, including the CEO. It requires a close collaboration between data and business teams, while at the same time, people and teams need to become data literate and adopt a statistical mindset.

- The aim is to get to a 'Prove it' culture based on scientific reasoning. This involves a process of claiming, evidence and reasoning. Evidence guides us to the truth by contributing to our beliefs.

- Enabling data and analytics requires a collective intelligence characterized by diverse opinions. It also takes alignment of different decision-maker types to ensure that judgments are properly informed and based on people's experience, expertise, skills and intuition, as well as data and analytics.

Putting It All Together to Improve Project Delivery Performance

"Nothing is impossible. The word itself says 'I'm possible.'"

— Audrey Hepburn

CHAPTER THIRTEEN

Engagement: Enabling Accountability and Transparency

Moving to a data-informed and evidence-based project management practice is a fundamental shift, but it does not have to be overly complex. The key to achieving a smooth transition is always the people, their mindsets, and behaviors adopting new ways of working to build a culture driven by knowledge and evidence. With a sound purpose following the key drivers and elements described in Part Two, people are more open to engaging in important change initiatives.

This engagement aims to drive commitment and accountability toward the following outcomes.

Collaborate across boundaries

- Actively share knowledge, information and data
- Take the value of data and knowledge seriously.

Adopt a growth mindset

- Be persistent in improving through experimentation, ideation, failure, learning and unlearning.
- Embrace uncertainty.

Establish a culture of candor

- Encourage authenticity and transparency.

This chapter takes a closer look at each of these outcomes.

....

Collaborate across boundaries

The discussion about improving collaboration is age-old. Cross-functional teams, removing silos, we have heard it all.

When we discuss boundaries in collaboration, it is usually all about hierarchical levels, functional/departmental boundaries, the exchange with externals such as vendors and clients, and geographic boundaries. Much is already written about it, so why bring it up here?

The key driver is to engage data and analytics, which should not downgrade any other collaboration efforts. Our goal is diligent knowledge management in the project management space. That includes exploring and integrating new and existing knowledge sources into an optimized and balanced knowledge mix. It requires active collaboration among people, teams and departments.

Cross-functional collaboration

Many organizations blend IT and business professionals in a model of cross-functional working with squads or agile pods. In doing so, they understand the importance of aggregating and reconciling relevant knowledge within the firm, which includes sharing data between teams and departments. Yet, according to Forrester, between sixty and seventy-three percent of all data within an enterprise goes unused by analytics.[1]

It should be clear by now that data is a key asset in the project management domain. It can detect hidden risks and any trends or patterns that indicate project slippage while providing insights into opportunities to improve project performance. This is evident in sharing project data with artifacts like project documentation, project plans, schedules, risk registers, decision logs and lessons learned. These crucial knowledge-sharing activities need to be standardized in the project organization.

Making tacit knowledge explicit

Data and analytics rely on explicit knowledge, but a large portion of knowledge is tacit. That covers intuitions and hunches based on a person's values, beliefs and experiences. None of which can be captured as explicit knowledge or data points.

We derive tacit knowledge through socialization and internalization (see figure 34).[2] In projects, a typical example is the onboarding of new team members. They go through existing documentation and artifacts to become familiar with the project and start practicing organization- and context-specific processes (internalization). Then there is a handover period of observing or shadowing peers (socialization).

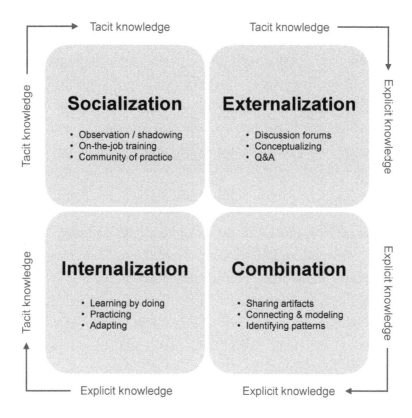

Figure 34: Knowledge conversion (adapted)[3]

Given that a significant chunk of knowledge assets is tacit (see Chapter Seven), our challenge is to make this explicit so we can combine it with other explicit knowledge artifacts and broaden the basis for operating analytics. Naturally, if more explicit knowledge is available, we can generate more accurate insights through analytics.

Externalizing tacit knowledge takes additional measures. These include enhanced collaboration between groups, project teams and subject matter experts, depending on where relevant knowledge and expertise reside in an organization. Introducing knowledge source maps could identify the right people and start engaging with them to externalize their tacit knowledge. Figure 35 shows an example of a knowledge source map.

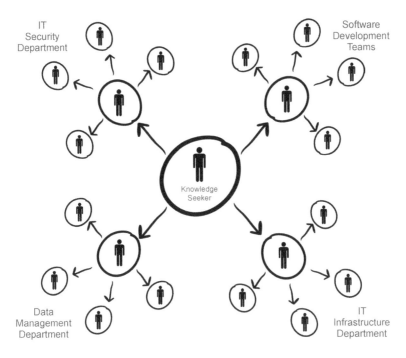

Figure 35: Example of a knowledge source map

The interactions involved in making intangible knowledge tangible are opportunities for discussion of mental models, concepts, metaphors and hypotheses. Although tacit knowledge cannot always be entirely explicit, the attempt to actively engage, share and exchange is worthwhile, as it eventually raises the bar of data quality and accuracy.

Actively share knowledge, information and data

There are many ways to actively share knowledge and make it accessible to the broader audience in an organization. The emphasis here is on active sharing, which goes beyond the mere storage or dumping of knowledge in a repository or knowledge management system (explicit knowledge) or being known for knowing something (tacit knowledge).

The measures in the following list can foster a culture of knowledge sharing.

Establish a community of practice

Active sharing means making the receiver aware that knowledge has been added and made accessible. It should trigger active learning and a mindset of proactively seeking answers or solutions.

Many organizations have a project management community based on voluntary participation. Establish a community of practice for project management professionals to learn, share and ensure collaboration between departments. This strengthens the bond between teams as the exchange and learning generate new knowledge.[4] Figure 36 illustrates this.

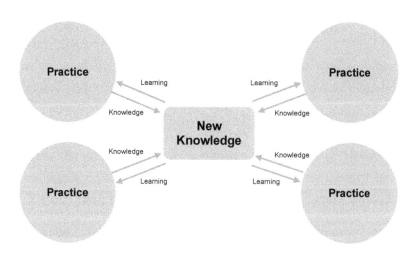

Figure 36: Community of Practice for knowledge sharing and building

A clear association with business results and an understanding of the shared knowledge's impact is most important. What value does the community of practice provide, and what are the precise outcomes or deliverables of sharing that knowledge?

Dan Ranta contributed a case study in the *Knowledge Manager's Handbook*.[5] He described how a global oil and gas company (Oilco) connected the desired behavior of knowledge sharing to business value. A community of practice provided a clear business case showing how a specific piece of knowledge contributed to business value. It triggered engagement from people who understood why they should invest time and knowledge sharing in such a community.

Build an expert database

Projects often need to access knowledge outside the team's expertise. For example, a project may have the scope to source and implement a new document management system for a specific business domain, and approach an external expert to understand how such systems work.

Someone may be looking for ideas of implementation methods for a particular type of project, let's say the upgrade of an ERP system. There are, of course, departments available for particular topics, such as agile coaches, but it is often unclear where to look, especially in larger organizations. Organizations have employee databases, so why not enhance those by capturing people's expertise from the projects and areas they have worked in? Again, a knowledge source map, as shown in figure 36 could be useful here.

You might find someone who developed a successfully implemented method to run a particular cloud migration initiative and has insights into specific challenges and risks. That person could volunteer to be available for an hour a week on an "Ask-me-anything" call to help solve somebody else's problem.

Rotate team members

Properly planned and prepared, rotating people across different project teams can be an effective tool to transfer tacit knowledge within the organization. Use competency analysis methods to identify specific knowledge transfer subjects, and the teams and people who would benefit most. Knowledge transfer can be targeted to specific needs, communication conditions, learning abilities, etc., raising the efficiency of tacit transfer.[6]

Incentivize knowledge sharing

Some organizations provide incentives for active knowledge sharing by linking it to annual performance reviews or bonus programs. That means people are rewarded for their efforts in sharing knowledge with other teams and departments.

Hold brown bag sessions

These sessions are often used to actively share knowledge and insights on a particular subject or project. Over a brown bag (provided) lunch, a project team might present its experience and learnings from a particular project. They cover the risks they faced, how they managed them and how they achieved their goals.

The downside of this approach is that it is usually based on project success stories rather than failures. The thinking is that if a project goes well, others should learn so they can bake the practices into their projects. However, failed projects have learnings as well. So, why not make a presentation about a project that failed and highlight what went wrong, as in a post-mortem exercise? This would be at least as informative and valuable as success stories.

> *Failed projects have learnings as well.*

The problem here is, of course, linked to people's views on success and failure. Few people want to volunteer to present their failure story, as it could be perceived as "Look how I've messed this thing up." Shame and guilt could dominate. This derives from an organizational culture based on reward and punishment, and motivates people to hide failures.

Reward knowledge sharing

What is important is that an organization builds a sharing culture aligned with trust, tolerance and reward.

People only share knowledge when they are sure it will not be used against them or disadvantage their standing in the organization. There must be a benefit or reward for the person who contributes to the organization's knowledge. This is especially true when sharing knowledge linked to failures. These rewards should be even greater as they provide insights that are often hidden due to feelings of shame or guilt.

Perceive knowledge differently

There's a problem though. We tend to treat knowledge like we own it, which reinforces resistance to sharing.

PART FIVE

No knowledge is ever truly our own.

While it is understandable that the investment of effort in gaining knowledge makes it feel like intellectual property, no knowledge is ever truly our own.[7] All knowledge is based on learning from others. We stand on the shoulders of giants.

Knowledge is, therefore, an evolutionary construct that doesn't reach an end state. It is constantly enhanced, reinforced and built upon. Leaders need to emphasize this way of thinking to drive knowledge sharing.

Adopt a growth mindset

Don't underestimate the need for growth thinking, especially with a transition to data-informed and evidence-based practices. With a fixed mindset, people are usually self-centered and focus more on their intelligence than the collective effort to improve the project management discipline.

When adopting a growth mindset, people become conscious of their strengths and weaknesses, recognize their gaps, and are more open to seeking and receiving feedback and being proven wrong.

In *Fail Fast, Learn Faster,* Randy Bean writes that failure is the foundation of innovation. Growth requires taking risks and investing in learning and failure.[8]

Celebrate failure

See failure as simply another set of insights. It is a source of learning and growth to be celebrated. It helps us look for solutions off the beaten path by identifying boundaries and strengthening messages.

A growth mindset actively promotes failure, but it requires a rethinking of organizational structures. If promotions are based on delivery success stories, then projects get pushed through, just to tick the "Delivered" box, regardless of value or whether the project should have been completed.

> *A growth mindset actively promotes failure.*

Years ago, I worked in the compliance domain of a bank. I took over an ongoing and already delayed project to deliver an in-house developed software application enhanced with functionality migrated from a legacy application. The goal was clear: get rid of the legacy application as it was outdated technology.

As the application was accessed by thousands of users in the bank, this critical project received great attention from senior management. It was particularly hot as the project had already been delayed. The project team was highly engaged, and there were generally good spirits to get the job done and deliver on target.

Stakeholder expectations were high, and deadlines were challenging, pushing the entire team to the edge, with long work hours that often included weekends. This was mainly due to various challenges with the chosen solution. Tests showed a working but relatively unstable and slow application, which could make the solution difficult for users. This almost guaranteed there would be complaints once it was live. But going back to the drawing board to work out more suitable solutions was not an option as it would have pushed the delivery date into the following year. Consequently, the project work was pushed to deliver by the expected date.

We delivered this multi-million dollar project after eighteen months or so of hard work. Everybody was relieved. We celebrated our success and were happy to have achieved such an important milestone. The hard work paid off.

So far, so good, and you might think that sounds like a success story. But approximately one year after the project delivery, the platform and application were abandoned and decommissioned, replaced by relatively cheap off-the-shelf software evaluated as more valuable in terms of operational cost and functionality.

What happened?

The delivery of that project was a critical performance goal for various people at various levels in the bank. It was even tied to some promotions, meaning that took precedence over a more reasonable goal: to deliver actual value. But there was no appetite to stop the project or take a different path because it would have meant postponing the delivery date, and the performance goal for that year wouldn't have been met.

In other words, fear of not meeting performance goals was the dominating factor that drove the project instead of acknowledging failure (a wrong solution) and investing in experimenting with potential other solutions.

What has that to do with becoming data-informed in projects? Rather a lot, actually.

Openness and an environment that doesn't condemn, sees failure as a requirement for growth and progress enabling higher transparency, authenticity and truthfulness. And that converts into new insights and long-term success.

As data-informed practices imply, failure is essential experimentation. Trying out various solutions builds knowledge for valuable insights.

> *Failure is essential experimentation.*

Be persistent

In a journey to data-informed practices, the initial results will probably be disappointing, but that is not linked to a technical setup or data quality problem. Leaders and decision-makers need to transition their minds and expectations to the new way of working. This doesn't happen quickly, as it takes practice to accept a mindset that internalizes new realities, such as the following:

- You might be wrong and may have to correct your views, even those deeply embedded in your expertise and knowledge.
- Accept answers you may not have expected, even if they do not match your preferences.
- Embrace challenges and risks. You may fail, but that generates new knowledge and improvement.
- Commit to learning.

PART FIVE

The important thing is to be persistent and not intimidated by initial struggles. With this in mind, keeping the team motivated can become a critical factor in this journey.

One approach to support motivation and engagement is frequently publicizing efforts and wins. That way, most of the organization knows the results being produced and recognizes the value of new project delivery practices using data and analytics. Richard Benjamins noted in his book *A Data-Driven Company* that such an approach can significantly impact team motivation as it drives awareness and highlights the importance of the invested efforts. This also increases the likelihood that senior managers recognize the value and further engage in such initiatives.[9]

Embrace uncertainty

Eventually, we all have to buy into uncertainty. We know that projects have to deal with it, and uncertainty is often regarded as the evil or the enemy, yet, surprisingly, it supports progress and helps us evolve.

We do everything possible to avoid uncertainty, including brainstorming solutions to eliminate it. But as it is a constant, we are always striving for excellence which drives progress and evolution. Embracing uncertainty means acknowledging this and continuously seeking a balance with knowledge.

If your goal is to eliminate uncertainty, you stop innovation, progress, development and evolution. You might even reverse what has already been achieved.

Think about it like going to the gym or doing exercise in general.

We all know that to stay healthy, we should exercise, work out, or do any kind of sport that trains muscles. Many people do so just to stay in good health, while others chase goals by going to the gym and lifting weights every day.

The first group of gym-goers is not interested in gaining muscle mass. They exercise to maintain the status quo of their health and fitness. The second group wants to progress. They are challenged every day because they continually increase the weights they lift.

There is a limit to how far a person can go in lifting weights, but that is exactly what uncertainty is about. We know there is a limit, but we don't know where it is, so we keep trying to improve our performance. We progress and evolve.

The truth, for both groups, is that there's a decline in performance when we stop exercising. All the effort it took to improve or reach a consistent level of performance is lost.

Uncertainty is the stressor we need to progress.

It helps us consider how we can reduce uncertainty to reach our goals. The result is that we come up with novel ideas, new thinking, and innovative solutions...continually.

> *Uncertainty is the stressor we need to progress.*

Embracing uncertainty is nothing more than acknowledging that we need it to progress and develop.

....

PART FIVE

Establish a culture of candor

A lack of transparency is a major blocker for a data-informed and evidence-based project management practice as it hides what is going on in a project, leading to inaccurate project data, potentially incorrect insights and even wrong decisions.

> *Transparency is a choice.*

Transparency is a choice, and it is a leader's responsibility to value and reward people's openness. And that requires an awareness of the usual impediments to transparency, as noted by Warren Bennis, Daniel Goleman and James O'Toole in their book *Transparency*.[10] We find some of the following in project environments.

Covering up mistakes

Many project teams are stretched and in firefighting mode, so failures or wrong decisions are often skipped over, and teams move on to the next project (and possible failure).

Shame, guilt or ego mean mistakes are covered up instead of learned from.

But postmortems or lessons learned are deeply valuable pieces of knowledge-building and learning exercises, and should never be skipped.

Tailored messages

We adjust our message and communication style based on the person we are talking to. Speaking with a peer is usually very different from communicating with your supervisor. The message is often softened or colored to make it more digestible to the person in power.

Most leaders know they receive an edited version of a message, so they must promote a culture that internalizes what we usually refer to as "speaking truth to power". This opens doors for people to tell their boss what they are doing wrong or what they should do differently.

Hoarded information

Some project managers actively block sharing information for competitive reasons. They may be part of a group of project managers and hoard information as a source of power. The often coined phrase "knowledge is power" finds application here. It's negative though, as power from knowledge means one person gains an advantage over others or is perceived as more knowledgeable.

Holding on to valuable knowledge and information can be costly. It impacts the goal of implementing data-informed practices as the creation and multiplication of knowledge and project data assets gets blocked. It also harms organizational efficiency and morale.

A technical solution to this problem is centralizing data in a single solution to unify data management. However, as mentioned earlier, a purely technical solution is often ineffective as data assets frequently require a fair amount of tacit knowledge to make complete sense. It is, therefore important to invest in measures to improve collaboration among departments, teams and employees. That might be by highlighting the value of sharing data and knowledge for the project management practice and the people therein.

Chapter takeaways

- Establishing enhanced collaboration among people and with data requires diligent knowledge management. That includes exploring and integrating new and existing knowledge sources into an optimized and balanced knowledge mix, and instilling a strong knowledge-sharing culture.

- A growth mindset accompanies the willingness for failure to drive innovation. The way to data-informed practices is full of challenges that are learnings and part of the journey to excellence. Persistence is key.

- A lack of transparency is a major blocker for a data-informed and evidence-based project management practice as it hides what is really going on, leading to inaccurate project data, potentially incorrect insights, and eventually wrong decisions.

CHAPTER FOURTEEN

Intelligence: Aggregate Knowledge

Data can be turned into information, knowledge and eventually wisdom. We can describe wisdom as intelligence as it includes reflection, the application of aggregated knowledge, and action in the form of decision-making and execution. It is ultimately where collected insights make an impact.

With optimized project management knowledge enabled by the behaviors described in Part Four, we can work towards the following characteristics.

Knowledge agility

- Be knowledge-driven, not data-driven.

Project resilience

- Explore scenarios and different futures.

Evidence-based thinking

- Use the best available evidence to make decisions.

....

Knowledge agility

In the transition to data-informed project delivery practices, knowledge agility is the ability to maintain the best available current knowledge for accurate decision-making. It is driven by a fundamental understanding that knowledge is dynamic and changes over time. That is true today more than ever.

Knowledge agility is characterized by the ability to quickly acknowledge, update and effectively use changes in our existing understanding. It requires a mindset of constant exploration and experimentation, and a readiness to act on the updated knowledge. Knowledge agility also relies on the effective collaboration of data, experience and intuition. Each complements the other in generating insights that project teams can act upon.

Be knowledge-driven, not data-driven

The term "data-driven" comes up sooner or later in every discussion around digital transformation, innovation and making use of data. What does it mean? According to Carl Anderson, it means "building tools, abilities, and, most crucially, a culture that acts on data."[1]

In *Be Data Literate,* Jordan Morrow refers to a data-driven culture in companies where data and analytics are taken seriously. When people become data literate, they develop a mindset of challenging assumptions and recognize that data has a stake in decision-making processes.[2]

It is an overarching term that indicates the significance of data. It's not as though we have never used data; we collect it to back up our assumptions whenever we make decisions.

Data-driven means something else. It is not about reinforcing hypotheses and subjective views that we know are heavily biased and usually incorrect. Right now, we need data to challenge us and our views. Hence, the expression "data-driven" highlights that data is more than just data. It gets a vote that needs to be taken seriously in our judgments.

The problem is that we don't always understand that, so we take it to the extreme. Giving data a vote doesn't mean that data has a voice. We enable data to have a voice through data literacy. We retrieve insights from data based on data literacy skills, helping us make better judgments.

> *Giving data a vote doesn't mean that data has a voice.*

Let's put this into the context of project management. Whenever I debate with project management practitioners, many question the suitability of data-driven practices in projects. Their key argument is usually that data cannot drive project decisions as it lacks emotional intelligence in a people-centered discipline like project management.

It's a valid point.

Many decisions are based on tacit knowledge, experience and intuition, which cannot be captured as measurable data points. If you are putting a project team together for a software development project, you'll choose the best performing software developers based

PART FIVE

on their seniority level, references and past performance reviews. Does that make it a winning team? Not always.

People need to collaborate and work as a team, and often there are gaps in the cultural fit that could cause conflict and harm project performance. Project managers make these decisions based on their experience and conflict management skills.

> *Projects are driven by more than just data.*

In other words, projects are driven by more than just data. Unfortunately, popular terms like "data-driven" and "single source of truth" give the impression that data is the leading force that either confirms or disproves our views. People who are not data-literate think that data is always right and drives decisions. This is a dangerous interpretation.

Data and analytics complement people's experience and intuition toward the best possible knowledge. Biases and irrational behaviors strongly influence intuition and behaviors, but data analytics can uncover those flaws and close the gap. At the same time, data lacks emotional and behavioral metrics. Driving projects to success requires leadership, relevant experience and skills that enable leaders to choose the right words to inspire and lead their teams.

A data-informed setup combines the best of both worlds, which means the focus must be on knowledge and not on data alone. Making sense of the whole of knowledge is the art and the key to successful project performance. And this implies that knowledge must be built, maintained and continuously enhanced.

Become a knowledge gardener

Project management is an evolutionary discipline, so learning and knowledge gathering should never stop. Practically, we build knowledge with every project we undertake, adding knowledge on top of what we already know so we do not have to start from scratch.

In the end, value comes from the aggregation of knowledge. Unfortunately, this is often forgotten, and the evolution of project management stalls. Evolution is not an exercise in optimizing practices; it's about advancing, innovating and making them suitable for the environments in which they are applied.

> *Value comes from the aggregation of knowledge.*

The phrase "knowledge gardening" is particularly valid in the project management domain, as knowledge preservation is critical. No one can claim to be a complete project manager because that person doesn't exist. A project management professional has basic knowledge, which is useless unless they recognize that it constantly needs to be revalidated and enhanced with new insights.

The core principles of project management involve learning, gaining and preserving knowledge and immediately seeking new knowledge. It is a neverending cycle. Once you stop, you may as well give up your role as a project management professional as your knowledge garden will dry up and eventually die.

While this applies to every individual in the project management domain, the real value comes from combining knowledge gardens into a knowledge forest where everybody contributes to its growth and health.

An admittedly very simplified starting point could be as follows.

Capture knowledge in a knowledge management system

I know what you are going to say. "What? Really? This is nothing new...."

That's correct!

It's not at all new, and almost every company has one. But are you using it effectively in project management?

You probably store project management data, such as lessons learned, in a knowledge management system. But do all the project teams have access to it? And are they using it to get insights from other teams?

To get real value, project teams must make all their project artifacts available in an open and searchable system. It should not be limited to lessons learned or sprint information as, without additional information and artifacts, these may not be meaningful enough to be considered knowledge.

Categorize your data

To make such a repository of project information useful, it should follow a certain structure. Categorize information by the type of artifact, e.g., project schedules and risk registers. Do this by creating subfolders — just as you do on a file share or in your local project folder.

Ideally, categorization should be consistent, with a common structure defined for all projects across the organization.

What if your risk registers are maintained in an online system rather than stored in a file system? Post the link to the online system so anyone can find it easily.

Tag your data

Use tags and labels on all information going into your knowledge management system. Many organizations use systems such as Atlassian Confluence, where you can label any page. This helps in searches for relevant knowledge.

Imagine you are working on a data migration project which includes Microsoft Sharepoint. You could search in your Confluence system for labels such as "data_migration" and "Sharepoint" and then get a list of projects that meet those criteria. This narrows the search to relevant projects and information, as you are extracting the signal and eliminating the noise. You can then retrieve valuable insights to help plan your project.

Obviously, the key is tagging information appropriately, with consistent labels that are valid for all projects across an organization.

Ideally, all information stored should follow a consistent format. That way, you can eventually use intelligent tools for in-depth analysis of the knowledge database. Good project data organization will eventually help you to run meaningful reports, and analytics in popular tools such as Power BI, Tableau, or Qlik Sense, to gain insights across projects and generate recommended actions.

Your project management practice, and eventually your projects, will benefit from knowledge gardening. You are maintaining your garden, keeping plants healthy and growing while also planting new seeds that will ultimately provide value and let your knowledge garden grow into a forest.

Preserving knowledge is the key to nurturing and harvesting your garden.

....

Project resilience

In Part Four of the book, we examined how our understanding of project resilience has changed from bouncing back from adversity, to a bag full of possible scenarios for possible redirection.

Work with scenarios and different futures

Today's business dynamics leave project leaders with no option except to reverse engineer the future.

Instead of being reactive to new technologies, we need to look ahead, imagine the future, and plan the steps to get us there. We must apply long-term strategic thinking to be ahead of any disruptions.

Conduct a pre-mortem

One way to generate useful information is through pre-mortem workshops. These are similar to post-mortem workshops, except they involve analyzing what contributed to the failure of a project. While a post-mortem takes place at the end of the project, the pre-mortem workshop happens at the beginning.

Team members and stakeholders simulate a project failure and work out why the project could have failed. It's a useful and often enlightening exercise that complements an approach I call *Planning to Fail*.

The concept is simple.

Create a project plan, a work breakdown structure (WBS), with the aim of running the project into the ground. Think hard about what needs to happen to make it fail. What roadblocks, issues and problems could you throw in the way that will guarantee failure? It sounds like a fun exercise — and it is, especially for team members who usually see everything entirely negatively and believe projects are doomed from the start.

This exercise invites participants to come up with all kinds of failure scenarios, from worst-case and extreme, to obvious risks. Build various plans and sequences that would cause the project to fail, then prioritize these to work out mitigation plans.

Alongside this experience and intuition-focused exercise, we can use historical project data and insights to model specific risk scenarios. Depending on the detail of available information, we may even be able to simulate certain situations to understand their impact better. Based on this collective view of failures, we can determine which strategies would be most appropriate to address possible futures.

The essential point, though, is to become aware of the possibilities. If they occur, we've already considered them and may even have pre-empted them with a response strategy. This is how we train resilience muscles, building in an adaptive capacity combined with a suitable degree of informedness.

Strategic and predictive thinking

The learning element in projects has become important in recent years. And with more frequent disruptions expected in the future, we must learn from experience and develop and strengthen capabilities to get a better grasp of possible threats or opportunities. This is what Rita McGrath, strategic management scholar and professor of management at the Columbia Business School, calls "seeing around corners."[3]

Many project teams react rather than prevent or mitigate when hit by unforeseen events and surprises. Again, COVID-19 should serve as an eye-opener because projects and organizations were unprepared for the implications of lockdowns.

Some organizations had no way to respond adequately and eventually had to shut down their operations. Other organizations took precautionary measures and had a Plan B in the drawer. They knew how to cope when everybody had to work from home instead of from the office.

We must become better at interpreting the signs.

A pandemic of this magnitude had not happened in living memory, but there were indications and signs, so it could have been predicted to some extent.[4] COVID-19 has demonstrated that we must become better at interpreting the signs and become more resilient. The future is guaranteed to hold more surprises and disruptions.

How we deliver projects in the future will be defined by how fast we can adapt to new demands and execute accordingly. Inevitably, this requires project professionals to engage in more scientific and statistical thinking to effectively use data and analytics towards better cost estimation and budget forecasting in project management and improved resource utilization. As we discussed in Part One, the project management discipline is lagging behind in this.

....

Evidence-based thinking

Scientific and statistical thinking concepts are directly linked to evidence-based practices as they add logic and facts, potentially revealing thinking errors or even complete nonsense.

In her book *Prove it!,* performance measure specialist Stacey Barr noted that evidence can be both a tool in our hands and a rod for our backs.[5] In projects, evidence helps us learn more about our true performance while unearthing impediments and breaking open the truth.

The price is transparency and accountability, as highlighted in the previous chapter.

Use the best available evidence to make decisions

Based on the concepts described in Part Three, project leaders and decision-makers can improve the quality of their decisions by rigorously applying an evidence-based mindset and thinking, ensuring that the best available evidence is used as a basis.

But generated evidence needs to be used rigorously and continually. Stanford professors Robert Sutton and Jeffrey Pfeffer noted in their book *Hard Facts, Dangerous Half-Truths, and Total Nonsense* that people often don't want to hear the truth or simply cannot handle it.[6]

We like to talk about success stories, not failures. And we don't want to be the messenger for bad news — if that is what the truth is.

It comes down to the culture of candor, where people have no barriers to telling the truth and where every recipient is open to accepting it.

Chapter takeaways

- Knowledge agility acknowledges that the best available knowledge leading to most accurate decision-making is achieved through the right balance of data and analytics, experience and intuition. It is characterized by the ability to quickly adapt to changes in our existing knowledge, update and use it effectively.

- Measures like pre-mortem workshops and strategic and predictive thinking techniques can help to achieve project resilience using available knowledge, including data and analytics.

- Improve the quality of decisions by rigorously applying an evidence-based mindset and thinking, with the best available evidence as the basis.

CHAPTER FIFTEEN

Capability: Achieve High Performance

The ultimate goal of changing to data-informed and evidence-based practices in projects is to raise the bar in terms of the project team's capabilities. We want to continually and effectively meet the project client's demands, and fulfill the overall purpose of a project and the project management practice.

This is where you should see results, as improved capability means higher productivity, greater accuracy, better performance and increased customer satisfaction. Essentially we have put all the wheels in motion to achieve the following improvements:

Delivery

- Delivering true business value rather than merely output from projects
- Turning insights into action and impact.

Strategy alignment

- Working on the right projects

- Working with the right people.

Continuous improvement

- Synchronous and coordinated growth of delivery capabilities for ongoing high performance
- Advancing innovation capability.

Let's consider each of these in turn.

....

Delivery

The primary goal is delivery effectiveness which means delivering the truest and best value to project clients, on time, on budget, and per the agreed scope. This is achieved by filling the knowledge gaps that cause bad decision-making and project failures.

With the measures discussed in the different parts of the book, we establish a purpose that should serve as the North Star for the journey to adopt and transition to data-informed practices. It ensures that people engage in the journey and are locked into innovation and continuous improvement while delivering meaningful change to business customers.

Deliver true business value not just output

A sound purpose should constantly remind us that the end goal is effective delivery that provides genuine value to the business. The immediate effect of this transformation of project management practices is to deliver real value. Decisions are informed and rational, and teams become more adaptive, resulting in a project delivery practice with better effectiveness and performance.

We should not randomly address improvement areas as the focus should be on valuable project outcomes. Instead, we tailor the transformation to the most burning and underperforming elements.

For example, if projects are frequently delivered over budget, financial management could be seen as the most notable pain point and should take priority.

It doesn't make sense to focus on identifying, collecting and analyzing data related to scheduling and task estimation if the burning issue is related to resource management and project staffing.

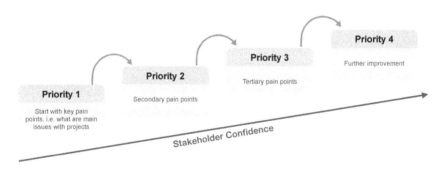

Figure 37: Prioritizing project management pain points to build stakeholder confidence

That is particularly true at the beginning of a transformation journey, where quick wins are needed to ensure continued executive management support toward a data-informed project management practice.

As figure 37 shows, it is essential to set the right priorities to ensure senior management stays confident that the investment in this transition is worthwhile.

PART FIVE

Such transformations could go horribly wrong if not carefully thought through or if managers carry the wrong expectations.

The right starting point

As we've established, some seventy percent of transformations to become data-driven fail. This should be a resounding warning to anyone starting this journey.[1]

Think about it. Data analytics is trendy. Everybody wants to boast that they are data-driven. But don't jump on it like winning the lottery and going on a wild spree. You can get it very wrong if you are not properly set up, not ready for it, or believe it will magically resolve all your project delivery issues.

That's why I emphasize that it's better to remove the term data-driven from your vocabulary. This misleading term has become a buzzword that easily gets attention, mainly because it stands for being innovative and modern rather than for the best reason of improving performance. In other words, use data and analytics to raise the bar of intelligence, capability and performance in projects, not just because everyone is talking about it. Otherwise, it will set the wrong expectations and likely end in failure.

Understand first where you are in your project management practice. How mature are your practices? What does your governance look like? Are your teams constantly firefighting their way through projects? Do you think bringing in a data analytics team to help with those issues will catapult your practice to delivery excellence?

Think again.

Undertaking a journey to data-informed practices starts with a shift in mindset and behaviors and requires preparing the ground for data and analytics to be useful.

Use **data to improve, not to fix**

It is fair to say that using data to gain new insights helps project management professionals better forecast and plan their projects.

And while that is true, it suggests that we are relatively good or at least ok-ish at bringing our projects across the finish line and providing decent value. Take another look at the survey results I referred to in the first chapter. The project management business is far from good, and what we've done so far has been somewhat mediocre. Don't get me wrong, many projects are exceptional, perfectly delivered, and a masterpiece of good project management. Perhaps the word *exceptional* summarizes the dilemma. When delivering projects, success should be the rule, not the exception. They should be the norm, not stand out. The problem is that most projects are not meeting expectations. Success rates of thirty to forty percent are unacceptable.

> *Success should be the rule, not the exception.*

Having a realistic understanding of your current project management practice is critical in deciding if you are in a position to transition to data-informed practices. You're not in good shape for transformation if your projects usually run at the edge with teams in firefighting mode, racing from project to project, with no time to do proper documentation or lessons learned.

PART FIVE

Data and analytics take your project management practice to the next level of improvement. It's like having a pacemaker implanted. But you cannot show up to the operation needing cardiac resuscitation. You have to stop the bleeding and stabilize the patient before surgery. We don't apply data analytics in project management to revive a dying patient. It is to support and improve the critical functions of your practice.

Data and technology are enablers

Data and technology are not machines or robots that take over project management work. They are innovative resources to help and support project managers and teams address their natural gaps. Something that cannot be resolved with traditional methods of experience or applying particular techniques or mental models.

Data and technology should be seen as enablers, not as tools. They complement existing knowledge in the project management space to improve performance.

In the pacemaker analogy, you must follow instructions to make the device work and ensure the operation is successful. You must be fit for surgery, and allowing for some pain, there will be a recovery period, and you may require a respirator to support your breathing.

For data analytics to be effective and shift the project delivery function to a high-performing practice, you may have to go through a stabilization phase before data-informed practices impact the business.

Turning insights into action and impact

We ultimately expect an impact from a new approach to project delivery. Data and analytics generate new knowledge, but insights need to be turned into action to unfold the power of knowledge. Data and knowledge are practically useless if not converted into insights and actions. As Wayne Eckerson says, "an actionable insight that no one acts on is worthless."[2]

A typical challenge in data-driven environments is that we have sufficient knowledge in the form of data, experience and intuition, and can analyze it to produce actionable insights, but there is no resulting action or impact on the project.

Don't lose sight of the overall goal and purpose. The leader's role is to keep reminding everyone of the project goal and business objective.

With this in mind, it is tempting to get carried away with all the new insights derived from data analysis. They are useless unless they are actionable or produce results. Insights need to be in a usable form that can change the project, for example, by influencing a decision.

....

Strategic alignment

We can change the project management domain in many ways, but transformation only makes sense if it provides value and contributes to growth and improved results.

Strategic alignment means different elements in an organization are arranged and coordinated to serve the defined purpose of the organization.[3]

As highlighted in Part One of the book, it comes down to true business value by delivering on defined goals and building an anticipative capability to gain competitive advantage.

A. G. Lafley, former chairman and CEO of Procter & Gamble, and Roger Martin, strategy advisor and former dean at the Rotman School of Management , University of Toronto call it "playing to win." In their book of the same name, they highlight that strategy is about winning choices. It's an integrated view of what you want to achieve, which field or market you are targeting, how you will win in that field, what capabilities are required, and which systems support it.[4]

For example, a bank's compliance department's vision/mission might say: "We want to ensure adherence to applicable regulations and policies while maximizing available resources to form the most effective and efficient methods to achieve and maintain regulatory compliance."

The key question is, "How can we do that?"

While there would likely be various considerations in answering this question, our focus is primarily on project management and its contribution to the vision. Possible answers could be reducing the turnaround time of projects to implement regulatory-driven changes and the risk of missing regulatory deadlines. Or it could be lowering change implementation costs.

Questions eventually lead to new capabilities to increase performance and deliver projects effectively and efficiently. These could include the need for innovation, a better understanding of the compliance department's problems, and a more anticipative view to foresee possible issues or changes, by introducing data-informed practices.

Various systems would support the necessary capabilities. These could include upskilling and training staff, processes to enable and maintain new capabilities, systems to measure the expected outcomes, communication channels to ensure information cascades across all levels, and frequent strategy reviews and discussions.

This eventually achieves a continuous strategic alignment between business and project management functions.

Work on the right projects

The primary benefit is that people work on the right projects, and their efforts aren't wasted. IT functions are often downgraded to become order takers to business partners. This results from strategic misalignment as the IT project department is too often detached from the overall business vision and purpose.

Equally, project selection mustn't be a top-down approach. Too often, a more tactical view sees IT functions like a rental car. We use it when we need it, expect it to function without any problems, and, of course, we don't want to worry about maintenance. But skipping maintenance work inevitably builds up technical debt that results in decreasing productivity and higher costs.

A frequent strategic alignment review should ensure that this does not happen by aligning technical debt prioritization with business objectives.

Work with the right people

When aligning priorities between business and project delivery functions, ensure the right capabilities and competencies are still in place to meet the strategic goals.

This is especially important with a transition to data-informed practices, where the right mix of people ensures the right balance of business knowledge, subject matter expertise, experience, data skills and intuitive intelligence. Some may think they need to build a data science team in projects to become data-informed. But what is needed is the right balance and distribution of knowledge to develop capabilities that align with the overall purpose and strategy.

Alignment is one of the most important terms in a transition to data-informed practices, as the new way of working requires continuous synchronization and coordination.

....

Continuous improvement

Throughout this book, I have described the importance of triggering the right mindset and behaviors. These enable data and analytics to improve project management performance and reach project delivery excellence.

But this cannot be a one-off event. Otherwise, teams return to their default mode, and nothing changes. Issues that have remained unaddressed for years have caused this current dilemma. You don't want to plant a garden, make it grow and prosper, collect the vegetables, then stop watering and let it die. You want to keep the garden growing. Keep building, and don't throw away what you have created.

Data is proof of what we create. It is an asset that needs to be nurtured and maintained. As Carruthers and Jackson write, "As people, we throw data away, only using it in hindsight to indicate past performance through management reports, scorecards, and dashboards, for example."[5]

However, most organizations still operate in the linear project economy model I described in Chapter Five. Valuable project knowledge is thoughtlessly thrown away and, with it, any opportunity for improvement.

It's all because the next project is waiting, and we have no time to pause. This is a high price to pay in the long run. It's a slow death, like being a chain smoker or an alcoholic. You don't feel the pain initially, but the longer it goes, the more negatively your health is affected. I was a heavy smoker for years in my twenties. I remember my mother saying, "You may not feel it now, but later you will feel the pain of what you have done to yourself." She was right, of course, and I am glad that I quit my addiction early enough.

Throwing away valuable data may not give you immediate pain, but it will later because you have missed accumulating knowledge.

In today's project world, the power is in capturing and building up knowledge, and making it available to everyone. The less you invest in exploring, maintaining and gathering knowledge from all available sources, the more effort and time each project will take. With today's fast pace, time is a luxury.

Synchronous and coordinated growth

Projects deliver change for clients, whether external or internal, like the finance or compliance departments. Either way, project success is determined by its value to the client's business.

The increasing pace of digitalization and the adoption of emerging technologies in all business areas means high dependency on technology change and its delivery. We rely far more on the respective team's capabilities to adapt quickly to change and deliver timely, accurately and efficiently. But projects often experience delivery delays as teams are not flexible or anticipatory enough to address the demand quickly and without delays. This is so despite the use of agile ways of working.

What is missing is a healthy and active innovation ecosystem across the entire project value chain, ensuring that new changes are addressed and rolled out quickly and effectively, according to the client's expectations and based on aligned capabilities.

Synchronized efforts for innovation between technology and project teams, change management, and business functions, can help to improve project performance and business effectiveness. In other words, it requires aligned strategies between project delivery functions and their respective business areas to avoid a capability gap that could lead to missed opportunities or failures.

This links to the organization's capability to execute its ambitions for continuous innovation. Innovation capability means the firm can generate and identify new ideas and use them for improved products, services, or processes, such as project delivery processes.[6]

Lawlor, O'Donoghue, Wafer and Commins elaborated on the need for an effective innovation ecosystem. They developed a framework that highlights the different dimensions for developing innovation capability within organizations: the strategy and vision of the business, the process, knowledge and competence, and the mindset of people.[7]

PART FIVE

272

It shows how a sound organizational vision that links with purpose can become a transformational tool that enables people to adopt new behaviors that support the required cultural change. It also drives people's willingness and motivation to learn and advance knowledge and competence. At the same time, the organization needs to provide the processes and structures to foster an environment of creativity, experimentation, and innovative thinking which develops and grows.[7]

This aligns strongly with the model that underpins this book. It seeks an interaction between purpose, behavior and knowledge to effectively use data and analytics in project management and raise delivery performance.

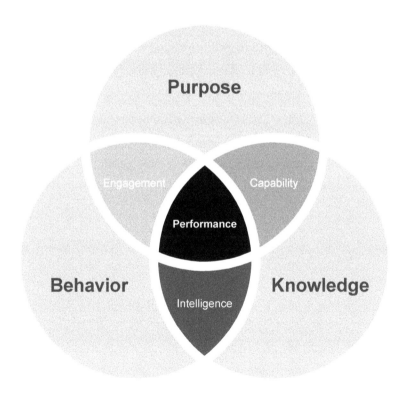

Figure 38: Achieving high project delivery performance

Building innovation capability is a key outcome of a transition to data-informed practices in projects. It provides a momentary lift in project performance that enables the dynamics and constant growth and change we generally see in business, and requires ongoing innovation and evolution.

Chapter takeaways

- The goal of producing valuable outcomes from projects also means applying a tailored approach of transitioning to data-informed practices by identifying the pain points and setting the priorities accordingly.

- The project management discipline must contribute to the organization's growth and improved results. That means continuous strategic alignment between business and project management functions.

- Synchronized efforts for innovation between technology and project teams, change management, and business functions, can help improve project performance and business effectiveness.

Conclusion

"Success is not a goal to reach or a finish line to cross. It is a system to improve, an endless process to redefine."

— James Clear

We acknowledge there are ongoing struggles to deliver projects effectively and provide value to project customers. And we have identified why we haven't seen much improvement in project success rates for a long time. So what is stopping us from addressing this problem? How can we turn the ship around and get into more manageable waters, away from constant heavy storms and turbulence?

In this book, I have highlighted the three main challenges that need addressing:

- Make faster and better project decisions
- Capture the information overflow
- Keep innovation strategies and capabilities in sync with business functions and technology.

Data analytics has long been on the radar for project management innovation, but few organizations have undergone the transformation. Instead, many are curious about advanced technologies like artificial intelligence (AI). But this is often the result of a misconception when people seek automation and believe that AI will magically resolve all their project management challenges. While AI will eventually play a role in the project management space, the first step must be to get comfortable with using data and analytics.

This challenge is often greater than anticipated because it requires different ways of thinking, decision-making and collaborating.

Revisiting the challenges and the points made throughout the book makes it clear that the most important asset in your project management toolset is knowledge — not data or technology.

Data is valuable, but it is only one ingredient of knowledge. While data and analytics help improve our knowledge, people's expertise, experience and skills play a crucial role. They outsmart data. Judea Pearl is a professor at the University of California who received the 2011 Turing Award for his contributions to probabilistic reasoning and causality. In *The Book of Why*, he wrote, "You are smarter than your data. Data do not understand causes and effects; humans do."[1]

You can call your project management practice data-driven, data-informed, data-centric, or whatever you like. But remember that true project delivery performance is based on constantly revising and growing knowledge into a capability that meets an organizational purpose.

As much as data improves project decisions, don't fall into the trap of focusing too much on it. Remember this, and your journey to a data-informed project management practice will be successful.

....

Next Steps

The question now is how to start such an important transformation journey.

The intention of this book was not to provide a manual to implement data-informed and evidence-based practices in your organization. That would have required far more technical detail.

Instead, this is a reminder that people and culture continue to play a major role in driving projects. We now have a tremendous opportunity to leverage data and analytics to our advantage, to become more effective and efficient.

We depend on people and culture to take that opportunity and on an effective interplay between purpose, behavior and knowledge. The rewards are worth the effort as they will open the doors to the future of project management.

There is no doubt that you will face challenges. Changing habits and behaviors is never an easy journey. Persistence, commitment and discipline are crucial to success. There will likely be some initial frustration from failed attempts to use data, and you may even fall back into old patterns. Project professionals know that fundamental changes bring initial setbacks.

Every organization, project environment, and culture has different characteristics, requiring a tailored roadmap of behavioral change toward data-informed practices. A transformation journey will have twists and turns based on the current state of a project management practice, the target destination and expected outcomes. Success depends on how ready an organization, its people, and its structures are to support a transformation. A highly traditional and hierarchy-focused organization functions very differently from a modern digital-savvy start-up. Like the various decision-maker types highlighted in Chapter Twelve (analytics-centered, old-fashioned, uncertain, balanced), organizational cultures have unique characteristics that need to be considered for a successful and effective transformation journey.

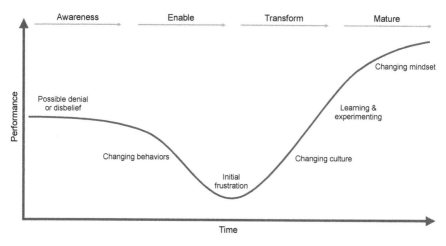

Figure 39: Transition roadmap

The following is a high-level overview of the transformation phases illustrated in figure 39.

Awareness

- Understand current issues in project delivery effectiveness, including fundamental behavioral and cultural gaps.
- Work out the steps necessary to improve the performance and outcomes of projects.

- Assess the project culture with a focus on possible psychological, social and cultural blockers for evidence-driven project management.
- Develop suitable measures to address them.

Enable

- Learn and practice new processes and techniques for improved resilience and collaboration.
- Build vision and purpose statements, and prioritize pain points in alignment with business goals.
- Build engagement and accountability for the transformation journey.

Transform

- Experiment with data in the context of decision-making.
- Establish processes and mindset for knowledge/data sharing and maintenance.
- Build stakeholder trust and confidence through initial quick wins (based on smaller project deliveries and/or proof of concept).

Mature

- Focus business and project delivery teams on strategic alignment to synchronize their capabilities in terms of innovation and overall goals.
- Strengthen and improve processes to retain and recycle project knowledge (circular project economy).

- Establish mechanisms to regularly review and advance established processes and practices, including introducing advanced technology.

I hope that by fully engaging in the necessary but rewarding journey to a data-informed project management practice, you will achieve fulfilment and success, evidenced by continuous value delivery in your project management practice. This book will help you to get started.

I would love to hear about your initiatives to transform your project delivery practice. Please be in touch. Send me an email at marcus@marcusglowasz.com, or visit www.marcusglowasz.com

About the Author

Marcus Glowasz is a project management professional and specialist with more than twenty-five years of experience in technology-driven projects. Over the last fifteen years, Marcus has specialized in highly data-driven transformation programs. This has primarily been in the regulatory compliance space within the financial services domain, where he has worked internationally  with large financial institutions such as UBS and Credit Suisse.

From his experience, research and resulting insights, Marcus developed an obsession with innovating and advancing the practice of delivering projects and change. He believes in the power of evidence-based practices to improve learning, enhance knowledge, and transform project management into a high-performing discipline.

Marcus co-founded Fortean, a Swiss technology startup that leverages artificial intelligence technology to support project management and delivery.

In recent years, Marcus has established his own business practice, working with organizations to plan and execute innovative change delivery strategies. Today, he runs programs internationally to help leaders and teams shift their change delivery and risk management practices to future-proofed, evidence-based and data-informed practices that align with today's rapidly changing business environments.

Marcus lives with his wife and two sons near Zurich, Switzerland.

You can find out more about Marcus at www.marcusglowasz.com or email him at marcus@marcusglowasz.com

Further reading

As this book provides an overview of behavioral and cultural challenges when transitioning to a data-informed project management practice, various areas and aspects are worth exploring in more detail. I have compiled a list of resources for readers who want to dive deeper into specific topics.

There is a wide range of literature, so the list is in no way exhaustive. In addition, as with project management practice, I recommend you constantly update yourself as new resources emerge, driving the development and further understanding of various topics.

Behavioral science

Ariely, Dan. (2013). *The (Honest) Truth About Dishonesty: How We Lie to Everyone — Especially Ourselves*. Harper Perennial.

Bennis, Warren, Goleman, Daniel & O'Toole, James. (2008). *Transparency: How Leaders Create a Culture of Candor*. Jossey-Bass.

Carucci, Ron A. (2021). *To Be Honest: Lead with the Power of Truth, Justice and Purpose*. Kogan Page.

Clear, James. (2018). *Atomic Habits: An Easy & Proven Way to Build Good Habits & Break Bad Ones*. Avery.

Edmondson, Amy C. (2018). *The Fearless Organization: Creating Psychological Safety in the Workplace for Learning, Innovation, and Growth*. Wiley.

Gigerenzer, Gerd. (2022). *How to Stay Smart in a Smart World: Why Human Intelligence Still Beats Algorithms*. Allen Lane.

Kahneman, Daniel. (2012). *Thinking, Fast and Slow*. Penguin Books.

Kahneman, Daniel, Sibony, Olivier & Sunstein, Cass R. (2021). *Noise: A Flaw in Human Judgment*. Little Brown Spark.

Maeda, John. (2020). *The Laws of Simplicity: Design, Technology, Business, Life*. MIT Press.

Mohajer, Sia. (2015). *The Little Book of Stupidity: How We Lie to Ourselves and Don't Believe Others*. CreateSpace Independent Publishing Platform.

Pfeffer, Jeffrey, & Sutton, Robert I. (2006). *Hard Facts, Dangerous Half-Truths And Total Nonsense: Profiting From Evidence-Based Management*. Harvard Business Review.

Schonthal, David, & Nordgren, Loran. (2021). *The Human Element: Overcoming the Resistance That Awaits New Ideas*. Wiley.

Data analytics

Davenport, Thomas H. & Harris, Jeanne G. (2017). *Competing on Analytics: The New Science of Winning*. Harvard Business Review.

Davenport, Thomas H., Morison, Robert & Harris, Jeanne G. (2010). *Analytics at Work: Smarter Decisions, Better Results*. Harvard Business Review.

Eckerson, Wayne. (2012). *Secrets of Analytical Leaders: Insights from Information Insiders*. Technics Publications, LLC.

Spalek, Seweryn. (2021). *Data Analytics in Project Management*. Routledge.

Vanhoucke, Mario. (2018). *The Data-Driven Project Manager: A Statistical Battle Against Project Obstacles*. Apress.

Data literacy

Jones, Ben. (2020). *Data Literacy Fundamentals: Understanding the Power & Value of Data*. Data Literacy Press.

Morrow, Jordan. (2021). *Be Data Literate: The Data Literacy Skills Everyone Needs To Succeed*. Kogan Page.

Decision-making

Bazerman, Max H. & Moore, Don. (2006). *Judgment in Managerial Decision Making*. 6th ed. John Wiley & Sons, Inc.

Duke, Annie. (2020). *How to Decide: Simple Tools for Making Better Choices*. Portfolio.

Kim, Nancy S. (2017). *Judgment and Decision-Making: In the Lab and the World*. Red Globe Press.

Schwartz, Barry. (2004). *The Paradox of Choice: Why More Is Less*. Ecco.

Virine, Lev & Trumper, Michael. (2019). *Project Decisions: The Art and Science*. 2nd ed. Berrett-Koehler Publishers, Inc.

Data storytelling and visualization

Duarte, Nancy. (2019). *DataStory: Explain Data and Inspire Action Through Story*. Ideapress Publishing.

Few, Stephen. (2012). *Show Me the Numbers: Designing Tables and Graphs to Enlighten*. Analytics Press.

Few, Stephen. (2021). *Now You See It: An Introduction to Visual Data Sensemaking*. Analytics Press.

McCandless, David. (2001). *Information Is Beautiful*. Collins.

Nussbaumer Knaflic, Cole. (2015). *Storytelling with Data: A Data Visualization Guide for Business Professionals*. Wiley.

Artificial intelligence

Anderson, Eric & Zettelmeyer, Florian. (2020). *Leading with AI and Analytics: Build Your Data Science IQ to Drive Business Value*. McGraw-Hill.

Boudreau, Paul. (2019). *Applying Artificial Intelligence to Project Management*. Independently published.

Daugherty, Paul R. & Wilson, H. James. (2018). *Human + Machine: Reimagining Work in the Age of AI*. Harvard Business Review.

Fry, Hannah. (2019). *Hello World: Being Human in the Age of Algorithms*. W.W. Norton Company.

Mohanty, Soumendra & Vyas, Sachin. (2018). *How to Compete in the Age of Artificial Intelligence: Implementing a Collaborative Human-Machine Strategy for Your Business*. Apress.

Shane, Janelle. (2021). *You Look Like a Thing and I Love You: How Artificial Intelligence Works and Why It's Making the World a Weirder Place*. Voracious.

Future thinking

Hines, Andy, & Bishop, Peter C. (2015). *Thinking about the Future: Guidelines for Strategic Foresight.* 2nd ed. Hinesight.

Johnson, Mark W. & Suskewicz, Josh. (2020). *Lead from the Future: How to Turn Visionary Thinking Into Breakthrough Growth.* Harvard Business Review.

Lustig, Patricia. (2017). *Strategic Foresight: Learning from the Future.* Triarchy Press.

Ramírez, Rafael & Wilkinson, Angela. (2018). *Strategic Reframing: The Oxford Scenario Planning Approach.* Oxford University Press.

Wright, George & Cairns, George. (2017). *Scenario Thinking: Preparing Your Organization for the Future in an Unpredictable World.* 2nd ed. Palgrave Macmillan.

Cognitive biases

Optimism bias

Optimism bias is common in project management and project decisions. It is a view or belief that the future will be much better, although the current reality and past events suggest something else. A typical example is when a project manager takes over a project which previously failed to get delivered and approaches it with an attitude of "It won't happen to me", suggesting previous shortfalls or mistakes won't happen again. This kind of thinking is often detached from reality and can lead to project failures.

We often explain cost overruns through scope changes, increasing complexity, and technology changes. But this is not always the case. And project managers need to plan for possible deviations based on the risk of change. Even then, projects are usually underestimated and overrun. One root cause for this is the optimism bias which can happen to anyone, including experienced project managers.

In projects, this usually leads to the planning fallacy.

Planning fallacy

The planning fallacy is where we underestimate how long it will take to complete a particular project task — even if evidence or experience tells us differently. We are often overly optimistic and blame other factors such as delayed start dates or sick days when things go wrong.

Optimism bias is unintentional and based on natural cognitive bias, which is difficult to remove. Planning fallacy can include political biases when we want to make a point, or follow certain political or individual interests. It intentionally underestimates project costs or timelines.

This can happen when project managers want to position themselves in an organization and push timelines.

Status quo bias

Status quo biases are characterized by statements such as "We always have done it that way, so why change?" They are similar to the loss aversion bias, which means people focus more on what they might lose than what they could gain.

Interestingly, despite how bad a project situation is, most people feel more comfortable knowing what to expect than with the unknown.

Let's say an analyst in a project team comes up with an idea to adopt a new, more efficient process that involves tools to effectively track requirements. The project manager turns down the idea based on, for example, cost, risk of failure, or simply because it costs too much time. But the manager hasn't analyzed it properly because of their resistance to change and because things seem good enough. It's all working, and they are afraid to jeopardize the situation. This is a status quo bias.

Confirmation bias

Confirmation bias is widespread in projects. It is when you favor a particular idea or solution and search for information and evidence that backs your preference, disregarding information that could offer a different direction.

One example could be a stakeholder who is unhappy with the selection of a project manager and asks colleagues about their prior experience with that person. Most people may have had a good experience and support the project manager, but a few negative experiences could confirm the stakeholder's opinion.

It is again a natural bias that appears in everyday life, especially during political elections. People tend to seek positive information on their favored candidates to put them in a good light and look for information that shows opposing candidates negatively.

So when we say informed decision-making, we mean including objective information and sources that are representative and not distorted by confirmation bias.

Groupthink

This is where individual thinking is lost in efforts to reach a consensus. There is pressure to comply with the majority view.

One way to avoid this is working as a group through the decision-making process so we do not start with an opinion from one person.

Another risk shows up in hierarchy-driven organization structures, where people go with the majority view to maintain group harmony. In this situation, the group goal is to find a consensus and make a decision. But if people in a group are less critical and have a higher risk appetite and tolerance, they might make a different decision individually than within a group.

This phenomenon requires the project manager's awareness to take measures to avoid scenarios that could impact rational decision-making.

There are various ways to address and mitigate groupthink. One measure is to gather enough information to make an informed decision and review that information critically to analyze alternatives properly.

Anchoring

Anchoring happens when a project manager gets attached to a piece of information. For example, when estimating a project task, an engineer might say, "Five days should be enough". The number becomes anchored as a benchmark, and all subsequent statements, negotiations, or decisions are centered around this first estimate.

Halo effect

The halo effect is a cognitive bias in which we tend to attribute good or bad qualities to someone based on an impression of other unrelated qualities. So what does that mean in project management?

Let's say you are interviewing someone for a test engineer role, and you feel that this person is intelligent and good enough for the job because they seem likable. Your judgment is distorted by something unrelated to the role. You've decided the person is nice, so you conclude they are also intelligent.

Sunk cost bias

The sunk cost bias or sunk cost fallacy describes a tendency to proceed with a project or a solution purely because a lot of effort or money has already been invested in it. People are hesitant to abandon it even though information and facts warrant a change in direction.

The last step in the decision-making process is to monitor the decision for its effectiveness and confirm that it produces the expected outcomes and benefits. A sunk cost bias is a constraint as it avoids change, even though a decision may prove unsuitable and incorrect.

In project management, this bias is responsible for many projects being kept alive when they should have been terminated.

References

Preface

1. Wikipedia. https://en.wikipedia.org/wiki/Fortis_(finance)
2. Rajesh Kumar, B. (2019). ABN AMRO Acquisition by RFS Holding. In Wealth Creation in the World's Largest Mergers and Acquisitions (pp. 131–135). Springer.
3. Fister Gale, S. (2010). BNP Paribas Fortis, Brussels, Belgium. PM Network, 24(8), 32–35.
4. Project Management Institute. (2020). *Pulse of the Profession 2020*. https://www.pmi.org/learning/thought-leadership/pulse/pulse-of-the-profession-2020
5. Association for Project Management, & Wellingtone Ltd. (2020). *The State of Project Management - Annual Survey 2020*.
6. Australian Institute of Project Management, & KPMG. (2020). *Project Delivery Performance in Australia*.

Chapter 1

1. Arthur, Charles. (2013). Tech giants may be huge, but nothing matches big data. The Guardian. https://www.theguardian.com/technology/2013/aug/23/tech-giants-data
2. Sondergaard, Peter. (2011). Gartner Research 2011. *Gartner Symposium/ITxpo*.

3. Kang, Cecilia, & Frenkel, Sheera. (2018). *Facebook Says Cambridge Analytica Harvested Data of Up to 87 Million Users.* New York Times. https://www.nytimes.com/2018/04/04/technology/mark-zuckerberg-testify-congress.html

4. Lapowsky, Issie. (2019). *How Cambridge Analytica Sparked the Great Privacy Awakening.* Wired. https://www.wired.com/story/cambridge-analytica-facebook-privacy-awakening/

5. Bean, Randy, & Davenport, Thomas H. (2019). *Companies Are Failing in Their Efforts to Become Data-Driven.* Harvard Business Review. https://hbr.org/2019/02/companies-are-failing-in-their-efforts-to-become-data-driven

6. Nieto-Rodriguez, Antonio. (2021). *The Project Economy Has Arrived.* Harvard Business Review. https://hbr.org/2021/11/the-project-economy-has-arrived

7. Project Management Institute. (2020). Pulse of the Profession 2020. https://www.pmi.org/learning/thought-leadership/pulse/pulse-of-the-profession-2020

8. *The Rise of the Project Economy.* (n.d.). Berkley Group. https://www.berkley-group.com/the-rise-of-the-project-economy/

9. McCullen, Aidan. (2021). *Undisruptable: A Mindset of Permanent Reinvention for Individuals, Organisations and Life.* John Wiley & Sons Ltd.

10. *The Project Economy: What it means for the world, business, and you (Transcript).* (2019). European CEO. https://www.europeanceo.com/business-and-management/the-project-economy-what-it-means-for-the-world-business-and-you/

11. Stone, Lance. (n.d.). *How Has Technology Changed the World Over the Past 20 Years.* OnTimeTech. https://www.ontimetech.com/blog/20-years/

12. Wignaraja, Kanni. (2020). *Six leadership lessons from COVID-19*. United Nations Development Programme. https://www.undp. org/blog/six-leadership-lessons-covid-19

Chapter Two

1. Haughey, Duncan. (2010). *A Brief History of Project Management*. ProjectSmart. https://www.projectsmart.co.uk/history-of-project-management/brief-history-of-project-management.php

2. Project Management Institute. (2020). *Pulse of the Profession 2020*. https://www.pmi.org/learning/thought-leadership/pulse/pulse-of-the-profession-2020

3. Wellingtone Ltd. (2020). *The State of Project Management - Annual Survey 2020*. https://wellingtone.co.uk/wp-content/uploads/2020/06/The-State-of-Project-Management-Report-2020-Wellingtone.pdf

4. Australian Institute of Project Management, & KPMG. (2020). *Project Delivery Performance in Australia*.

5. The Standish Group. (2015). The Standish Group Report. In *The CHAOS Report*.

6. Pratt, Mary. (2021). *Why IT projects still fail*. CIO. https://www.cio.com/article/230427/why-it-projects-still-fail.html

7. Project Management Institute. (2017). *Project Management Job Growth and Talent Gap 2017–2027*.

8. Nieto-Rodriguez, Antonio. (2021). *Project Management Handbook*. Harvard Business Review.

9. Project Management Institute. (2018). *Pulse of the Profession 2018*.

10. Wikipedia. https://en.wikipedia.org/wiki/Volatility,_uncertainty,_complexity_and_ambiguity

11. McKinsey & Company. (2019). *Decision making in the age of urgency*. https://www.mckinsey.com/~/media/McKinsey/ Business Functions/Organization/Our Insights/Decision making in the age of urgency/Decision-making-in-the-age-of-urgency. pdf

12. Virine, Lev, & Trumper, Michael. (2019). *Project Decisions - The Art and Science* (2nd ed.). Berrett-Koehler Publishers, Inc.

13. Reinsel, David, Gantz, John, & Rydning, John. (2018). *Data Age 2025: The Digitization of the World From Edge to Core.* International Data Corporation (IDC), sponsored by Seagate.

14. *Amazon Prime Air prepares for drone deliveries.* (2022). Amazon. https://www.aboutamazon.com/news/transportation/amazon- prime-air-prepares-for-drone-deliveries

15. Hardy-Vallée, Benoit. (2012). How to Run a Successful Project. *Gallup.* https://news.gallup.com/businessjournal/152756/run- successful-project.aspx

Chapter Three

1. Benjamins, Richard. (2021). *A Data-Driven Company: 21 lessons for large organizations to create value from AI.* LID Publishing Limited.

2. Bean, Randy. (2021). *Fail Fast, Learn Faster - Lessons in Data- Driven Leadership in an Age of Disruption, Big Data, and AI.* Wiley.

3. Why do most transformations fail? A conversation with Harry Robinson. (2019). *McKinsey & Company.* https://www. mckinsey.com/business-functions/transformation/our-insights/ why-do-most-transformations-fail-a-conversation-with-harry- robinson

Chapter Four

1. Beck, Randall, & Harter, Jim. (2015). *Managers Account for 70% of Variance in Employee Engagement.* Gallup. https://news.gallup.com/businessjournal/182792/managers-account-variance-employee-engagement.aspx

2. Nieto-Rodriguez, Antonio. (2021). *Does Your Project Have a Purpose?* Harvard Business Review. https://hbr.org/2021/10/does-your-project-have-a-purpose

3. PWC. (2016). *Putting Purpose to Work: A study of purpose in the workplace.* https://www.pwc.com/us/en/about-us/corporate-responsibility/assets/pwc-putting-purpose-to-work-purpose-survey-report.pdf

4. Harvard Business Review, & EY Bacon Institute. (2015). *The Business Case for Purpose.* https://assets.ey.com/content/dam/ey-sites/ey-com/en_gl/topics/digital/ey-the-business-case-for-purpose.pdf

5. Nadella, Satya. (2017). *Hit Refresh: The Quest to Rediscover Microsoft's Soul and Imagine a Better Future for Everyone.* Harper Business.

6. *2022 Purpose Power Index™: Zoom, Tesla and Rei Among Top Purpose-Driven Brands; Newcomers Include Pfizer, Google and Toyota.* (2022). The Wise Marketer. https://thewisemarketer.com/research/2022-purpose-power-index-zoom-tesla-and-rei-among-top-purpose-driven-brands-newcomers-include-pfizer-google-and-toyota/

7. Vermeulen, Freek. (2019). *Companies Don't Always Need a Purpose Beyond Profit.* https://hbr.org/2019/05/companies-dont-always-need-a-purpose-beyond-profit

8. Sinek, Simon. (2013). *Profit isn't a purpose, it's a result. To have purpose means the things we do are of real value to others.* https://twitter.com/simonsinek/status/350265758913277952

9. Quinn, Robert E., & Thakor, Anjan V. (2019). *The Economics of Higher Purpose: Eight Counterintuitive Steps for Creating a Purpose-Driven Organization.* Berrett-Koehler Publishers, Inc.

10. Steele, Mark D. (2019). *Projects on Purpose 2.0.* Old Elm Tree Press.

11. Nieto-Rodriguez, Antonio. (2021). *Project Management Handbook.* Harvard Business Review.

Chapter Five

1. Bean, Randy. (2021). *Fail Fast, Learn Faster - Lessons in Data-Driven Leadership in an Age of Disruption, Big Data, and AI.* Wiley.

2. Glowasz, Marcus. (2020). *Why Nobody Really Learns from 'Lessons Learned' in Projects.* The Project Office. https://theprojectoffice.org/why-nobody-learns-from-lessons-learned-in-projects-943c1aadca2a

3. Project Management Institute. (n.d.). What is Project Management? https://www.pmi.org/about/learn-about-pmi/what-is-project-management

4. Association for Project Management (APM). (n.d.). What is project management? https://www.apm.org.uk/resources/what-is-project-management/

5. Project Management Institute. (2013). *A Guide to the Project Management Body of Knowledge: PMBOK Guide* (5th ed.). Project Management Institute.

6. Lustig, Patricia. (2017). *Strategic Foresight.* Triarchy Press.

7. Cambridge Dictionary. https://dictionary.cambridge.org/dictionary/english/uncertainty

8. Hubbard, Douglas W. (2014). *How to Measure Anything, Third Edition - Finding the Value of "Intangibles" in Business*. Wiley.

9. Rumsfeld, Donald. (2002). *Unknown Unknowns*. Wikipedia. https://en.wikipedia.org/wiki/There_are_known_knowns

10. Kay, John, & King, Mervyn. (2020). *Radical Uncertainty: Decision-making for an Unknowable Future*. W.W. Norton & Company.

11. Taleb, Nassim Nicholas. (2010). *The Black Swan: The Impact of the Highly Improbable* (2nd ed.). Random House Publishing Group.

12. Hyatt, Michael. (2020). *The Vision-Driven Leader: 10 Questions to Focus Your Efforts, Energize Your Team, and Scale Your Business*. Baker Books.

13. Stiglitz, Joseph E., & Greenwald, Bruce C. (2015). *Creating a Learning Society: A New Approach to Growth, Development, and Social Progress*. Columbia University Press.

14. Dwyer, Tim. (2022). Knowledge shared is knowledge grown. *Building Services Engineering Research and Technology*, 43(3), 277–278.

15. Cunningham, W. (2001). *Manifesto for Agile Software Development*. agilemanifesto.org.

16. Bridges, Jennifer. (2018). *What's the Real Value of Project Management?* Projectmanager.Com. https://www.projectmanager.com/training/value-of-project-management

17. Project Management Institute. (n.d.). *What is Project Management?* https://www.pmi.org/about/learn-about-pmi/what-is-project-management

18. Meadows, Donella H. (2008). *Thinking in Systems: A Primer.* Chelsea Green Publishing Co.

Chapter Six

1. Project Management Institute. (n.d.). *What is Project Management?* https://www.pmi.org/about/learn-about-pmi/what-is-project-management

2. *Why are we likely to continue with an investment even if it would be rational to give it up?* (n.d.). The Decision Lab. https://thedecisionlab.com/biases/the-sunk-cost-fallacy

3. Flyvbjerg, Bent. (2021). *How Big Is Cost Overrun for the Olympics?* Towards Data Science. https://towardsdatascience.com/how-big-is-cost-overrun-for-the-olympics-46e803cbf7d5

4. Bondarik, Roberto, Pilatti, Luiz Alberto, & Horst, Diogo José. (2021). The 2014 FIFA World Cup in Brazil: the promised legacy was dribbled past. *International Journal of Sport Management and Marketing, 21*(1/2), 134–147.

5. Garcia-Navarro, Lulu. (2015). *Brazil's World Cup Legacy Includes $550M Stadium-Turned-Parking Lot.* NPR. https://www.npr.org/sections/parallels/2015/05/11/405955547/brazils-world-cup-legacy-includes-550m-stadium-turned-parking-lot

6. Weick, Karl E., & Sutcliffe, Kathleen M. (2007). *Managing the unexpected: Sustained Performance in a Complex World.* Jossey-Bass.

7. Spalek, Seweryn. (2021). *Data Analytics in Project Management.* Routledge.

8. Eckerson, Wayne. (2012). *Secrets of Analytical Leaders: Insights from Information Insiders.* Technics Publications, LLC.

9. Sundar, Arvindh. (2017). *Understanding Data Driven Design Thinking*. https://www.linkedin.com/pulse/understanding-data-driven-design-thinking-arvindh-sundar/

10. Schmarzo, Bill. (2020). *The Economics of Data, Analytics, and Digital Transformation*. Packt Publishing.

11. Eckerson, Wayne. (2012). *Secrets of Analytical Leaders: Insights from Information Insiders*. Technics Publications, LLC.

12. Poppendieck, Mary, & Poppendieck, Tom. (2003). *Lean Software Development: An Agile Toolkit for Software Development Managers*. Addison Wesley Professional.

13. Ramirez, Rafael, & Wilkinson, Angela. (2018). *Strategic Reframing: The Oxford Scenario Planning Approach*. Oxford University Press.

14. Burrus, Daniel. (2017). *The Anticipatory Organization: Turn Disruption and Change into Opportunity and Advantage*. Greenleaf Book Group LLC.

15. Curry, Andrew, & Hodgson, Anthony. (2008). Seeing in Multiple Horizons: Connecting Futures to Strategy. *Journal of Future Studies, 13*(1), 1–20.

16. Lustig, Patricia. (2017). *Strategic Foresight*. Triarchy Press.

17. Nieto-Rodriguez, Antonio. (2021). *Project Management Handbook*. Harvard Business Review.

Chapter Seven

1. Handzic, Meliha, & Bassi, Antonio. (2018). *Knowledge and Project Management: A Shared Approach to Improve Performance*. Springer.

2. Liew, Anthony. (2007). Understanding Data, Information, Knowledge And Their Inter-Relationships. *Journal of Knowledge Management Practice, 8*(2).

3. Burton-Jones, Alan. (2001). *Knowledge Capitalism: Business, Work, and Learning in the New Economy.* Oxford University Press.

4. Milton, Nick, & Lambe, Patrick. (2019). *The Knowledge Manager's Handbook.* Kogan Page.

5. Burton-Jones, Alan. (2003). Knowledge Capitalism: The New Learning Economy. *Policy Futures in Education, 1*(1).

6. Used with permission of SAGE Publications Ltd. Journals, from Burton-Jones, Alan. (2003). Knowledge Capitalism: The New Learning Economy. *Policy Futures in Education, 1*(1); permission conveyed through Copyright Clearance Center, Inc.

7. Collins. https://www.collinsdictionary.com/dictionary/english/experience

8. Gigerenzer, Gerd. (2008). *Gut Feelings: Short Cuts to Better Decision Making.* Penguin Books.

9. University of Leeds. (2008). *Go With Your Gut - Intuition Is More Than Just A Hunch, Says New Research.* ScienceDaily. https://www.sciencedaily.com/releases/2008/03/080305144210.htm

10. Lufityanto, Galang, Donkin, Chris, & Pearson, Joel. (2016). Measuring Intuition: Nonconscious Emotional Information Boosts Decision Accuracy and Confidence. *Psychological Science, 27*(5).

11. Jung, Carl G. (1923). *Psychological types: or, the psychology of individuation.* Kegan Paul, Trench, Trubner & Co., Ltd.

12. *Insight vs Learning.* (n.d.). WikiDiff. https://wikidiff.com/learning/insight

13. Cambridge Dictionary. https://dictionary.cambridge.org/dictionary/english/insight

Chapter Eight

1. Schmarzo, Bill. (2020). *The Economics of Data, Analytics, and Digital Transformation*. Packt Publishing.

2. Project Management Institute. (n.d.). *PMP*. https://www.pmi.org/certifications/project-management-pmp

3. Axelos. (n.d.). *PRINCE2*. https://www.axelos.com/certifications/propath/prince2-project-management

Chapter Nine

1. Cambridge Dictionary. https://dictionary.cambridge.org/dictionary/english/data

2. Gigerenzer, Gerd. (2008). *Gut Feelings: Short Cuts to Better Decision Making*. Penguin Books.

3. *Marketing In The Dark - Dark Data*. (2018). IBM. https://www.ibm.com/blogs/think/nl-en/2018/04/24/marketing-dark-dark-data/

4. *Checker Shadow Illusion*. (n.d.). Edward H. Adelson, Vectorized by Pbroks13. - Own Work, CC BY-SA 4.0. https://en.wikipedia.org/wiki/Checker_shadow_illusion

5. *Before Electronic Spreadsheets*. (n.d.). Andrews Accounting. https://andrewstaxaccounting.com/spreadsheets/

6. Jackson, Peter, & Carruthers, Caroline. (2019). *Data Driven Business Transformation*. Wiley.

7. Palmer, Michael. (2006). *Data is the new oil*. ANA Marketing Maestros. https://ana.blogs.com/maestros/2006/11/data_is_the_new.html

8. Walker, Derek H. T., & Christenson, Dale. (2005). Knowledge wisdom and networks: a project management centre of excellence example. *The Learning Organization, 12*(3), 275–291.

9. Flyvbjerg, Bent. (2006). From Nobel Prize to Project Management. *PMI® Research Conference: New Directions in Project Management.*

10. O'Driscoll, Brian. (n.d.). *Knowledge is knowing that a tomato is a fruit, wisdom is not putting it in a fruit salad.* https://www.sportsjoe.ie/rugby/brian-odriscoll-tomato-fruit-salad-quote-21192

11. Gutierrez, Jason. (2017). *The Difference Between Knowledge and Wisdom.* Better Humans. https://betterhumans.pub/the-difference-between-knowledge-and-wisdom-3ff97605287a

Chapter Ten

1. *Fake News, Misinformation and Finding the Truth.* (n.d.). Marshall University Libraries. https://libguides.marshall.edu/fake

2. Sloman, Steven, & Fernbach, Philip. (2018). *The Knowledge Illusion : The myth of individual thought and the power of collective wisdom.* Pan Macmillan.

3. Klein, Gary A. (2011). *Streetlights and Shadows: Searching for the Keys to Adaptive Decision Making.* Bradford Books.

4. Toffler, Alvin. (1984). *Future shock.* Bantam.

5. Wikipedia. https://en.wikipedia.org/wiki/There_are_known_knowns

6. Hillson, David. (2014). *The Risk Doctor's Cures for Common Risk Ailments.* Berrett-Koehler Publishers.

7. Buehler, Roger, Griffin, Dale, & Ross, Michael. (1994). Exploring the "Planning Fallacy": Why People Underestimate Their Task Completion Times. *Journal of Personality and Social Psychology, 67*(3), 366–381.

8. Kahneman, Daniel, & Tversky, Amos. (1979). Intuitive prediction: Biases and corrective procedures. *TIMS Studies in Management Science, 12.*

9. Flyvbjerg, Bent. (2021). *How Big Is Cost Overrun for the Olympics?* Towards Data Science. https://towardsdatascience.com/how-big-is-cost-overrun-for-the-olympics-46e803cbf7d5

10. Wikipedia. https://en.wikipedia.org/wiki/Berlin_Brandenburg_Airport

11. Fiedler, Jobst, & Wendler, Alexander. (2016). Berlin Brandenburg Airport. In Genia Kostka & Jobst Fiedler (Eds.), *Large Infrastructure Projects in Germany: Between Ambition and Realities* (pp. 87–145). Palgrave Macmillan.

12. Downie, Andrew. (2014). *Brazil World Cup stadiums 50 percent over budget: report.* Reuters.

13. Waldron, Travis. (2014). *Brazil Spent $1 Billion More On World Cup Stadiums Than Originally Planned.* Think Progress. https://archive.thinkprogress.org/brazil-spent-1-billion-more-on-world-cup-stadiums-than-originally-planned-430c07a93c32/

14. Weick, Karl, & Sutcliffe, Kathleen. (2007). *Managing the unexpected: Sustained Performance in a Complex World.* Wiley.

15. Schein, Edgar H. (1984). Coming to a New Awareness of Organizational Culture. *MIT Sloan Management Review.* https://sloanreview.mit.edu/article/coming-to-a-new-awareness-of-organizational-culture/

16. Mikkelsen, Mogens Frank, Marnewick, Carl, & Klein, Louis. (2020). On Stupidity in Project Management - A critical

reflection of PM in a VUCA world. *The Journal of Modern Project Management, 8*(2).

Chapter Eleven

1. Pfeffer, Jeffrey, & Sutton, Robert I. (2006). *Hard Facts, Dangerous Half-Truths, and Total Nonsense*. Harvard Business Review.

2. Gigerenzer, Gerd. (2008). *Gut Feelings: Short Cuts to Better Decision Making*. Penguin Books.

3. Schmarzo, Bill. (2020). *The Economics of Data, Analytics, and Digital Transformation*. Packt Publishing.

4. *A New Way Of Thinking: Not Either-Or, But Both-And*. (n.d.). The Growth Equation. https://thegrowtheq.com/a-new-way-of-thinking-not-either-or-both-and/

5. Dweck, Carol. (2017). *Mindset*. Robinson.

6. *Total Number of Banks in the R3 CEV Blockchain Consortium Rises to 42*. (2021). Prove. https://www.prove.com/blog/total-number-of-banks-in-the-r3-cev-blockchain-consortium-rises-to-42

7. Kutsch, Elmar, Hall, Mark, & Turner, Neil. (2015). *Project Resilience: The Art of Noticing, Interpreting, Preparing, Containing and Recovering*. Gower Publishing Ltd.

8. Seville, Erica. (2016). *Resilient Organizations: How to Survive, Thrive and Create Opportunities Through Crisis and Change*. Kogan Page.

9. Morris, Jason. (2017). *What is a KYC analyst?* International Compliance Association (ICA). https://www.int-comp.org/insight/2017/december/what-is-a-kyc-analyst/

Chapter Twelve

1. Few, Stephen. (2019). *The Data Loom: Weaving Understanding by Thinking Critically and Scientifically with Data*. Analytics Press.

2. Morrow, Jordan. (2021). *Be Data Literate: The Data Literacy Skills Everyone Needs To Succeed*. Kogan Page.

3. Few, Stephen. (2019). *The Data Loom: Weaving Understanding by Thinking Critically and Scientifically with Data*. Analytics Press.

4. Harford, Tim. (2021). *The Data Detective: Ten Easy Rules to Make Sense of Statistics*. Riverhead Books.

5. Kahneman, Daniel. (2011). *Beware the 'inside view.'* McKinsey Quarterly. https://www.mckinsey.com/business-functions/strategy-and-corporate-finance/our-insights/daniel-kahneman-beware-the-inside-view

6. Flyvbjerg, Bent. (2006). From Nobel Prize to Project Management. *PMI® Research Conference: New Directions in Project Management*.

7. Servranckx, Tom, Vanhoucke, Mario, & Aouam, Tarik. (2021). Practical application of reference class forecasting for cost and time estimations: Identifying the properties of similarity. *European Journal of Operational Research*, 295(3).

8. Eder, Anna-Maria A., & Brössel, Peter. (2019). Evidence of Evidence as Higher-Order Evidence. In *Higher-Order Evidence - New Essays*. Oxford University Press.

9. Hedden, Brian, & Dorst, Kevin. (2021). (Almost) All Evidence is Higher-Order Evidence. https://philarchive.org/archive/HEDAAE-2

10. Horowitz, Sophie. (2014). Epistemic Akrasia. Noûs, 48(4), 718–744.

11. Collins. https://www.collinsdictionary.com/dictionary/english/evidence

12. Pfeffer, Jeffrey, & Sutton, Robert I. (2006). *Hard Facts, Dangerous Half-Truths, and Total Nonsense.* Harvard Business Review.

13. Ries, Eric. (2017). *The Lean Startup : How Constant Innovation Creates Radically Successful Businesses.* Currency.

14. IDEO | Global Design & Innovation Company | This Work Can't Wait n.d., cantwait.ideo.com.

15. Malone, Thomas W., & Bernstein, Michael S. (2015). *Handbook of Collective Intelligence.* MIT Press.

16. Surowiecki, James. (2005). *The Wisdom of Crowds.* Abacus.

17. Malone, Thomas W., & Bernstein, Michael S. (2015). *Handbook of Collective Intelligence.* MIT Press.

18. Hunt, Dame Vivian, Layton, Dennis, & Prince, Sara. (2015). *Why diversity matters.* McKinsey & Company. https://www.mckinsey.com/capabilities/people-and-organizational-performance/our-insights/why-diversity-matters

19. Gressel, Simone, Pauleen, David J., & Taskin, Nazim. (2020). *Management Decision-Making, Big Data and Analytics.* Sage Publications Ltd.

20. Used with permission of SAGE Publications Ltd. Books, from *Management Decision-Making, Big Data and Analytics*, Gressel, Simone, Pauleen, David J., & Taskin, Nazim, 2020; permission conveyed through Copyright Clearance Center, Inc.

21. Few, Stephen. (2012). *Show Me the Numbers: Designing Tables and Graphs to Enlighten.* Analytics Press.

22. Few, Stephen. (2021). *Now You See It: An Introduction to Visual Data Sensemaking.* Analytics Press.

23. Klein, Gary A. (2011). *Streetlights and Shadows: Searching for the Keys to Adaptive Decision Making*. Bradford Books.

24. Gressel, Simone, Pauleen, David J., & Taskin, Nazim. (2020). *Management Decision-Making, Big Data and Analytics*. Sage Publications Ltd.

Chapter Thirteen

1. Gualtieri, Mike. (2016). *Hadoop Is Data's Darling For A Reason*. Forrester. https://www.forrester.com/blogs/hadoop-is-datas-darling-for-a-reason/

2. Nonaka, Ikujiro, & Konno, Noboru. (1998). The concept of "ba": Building a foundation for knowledge creation. *California Management Review*, 40(3), 40–54.

3. Nonaka, Ikujiro, & Konno, Noboru (1998). The concept of "ba": Building a foundation for knowledge creation. *California Management Review, 40*(3), pp.40–54; copyright © 1998 by SAGE Publications. Used with permission of SAGE Publications.

4. Laufer, Alexander, Little, Terry, Russell, Jeffrey, & Maas, Bruce. (2017). *Becoming a Project Leader : Blending Planning, Agility, Resilience, and Collaboration to Deliver Successful Projects*. Palgrave Macmillan.

5. Milton, Nick, & Lambe, Patrick. (2019). *The Knowledge Manager's Handbook : A Step-by-Step Guide to Embedding Effective Knowledge Management in your Organization*. Kogan Page.

6. Lu, Honglei, & Yang, Congjie. (2015). Job Rotation: An Effective Tool to Transfer the Tacit Knowledge within an Enterprise. *Journal of Human Resource and Sustainability Studies*, 3(1), 34–40.

7. Jean-Pierre, Tavian. (2022). *Why You Should Always Seek to Share Your Knowledge*. DataDrivenInvestor. https://medium. datadriveninvestor.com/why-you-should-always-seek-to-share-your-knowledge-1102e700e995

8. Bean, Randy. (2021). *Fail Fast, Learn Faster - Lessons in Data-Driven Leadership in an Age of Disruption, Big Data, and AI*. Wiley.

9. Benjamins, Richard. (2021). *A Data-Driven Company : 21 lessons for large organizations to create value from AI*. LID Publishing Limited.

10. Bennis, Warren, Goleman, Daniel, & O'Toole, James. (2008). *Transparency: How Leaders Create a Culture of Candor*. Jossey-Bass.

Chapter Fourteen

1. Anderson, Carl. (2015). *Creating a Data-Driven Organization*. O'Reilly.

2. Morrow, Jordan. (2021). *Be Data Literate: The Data Literacy Skills Everyone Needs To Succeed*. Kogan Page.

3. McGrath, Rita Gunther. (2019). *Seeing Around Corners: How to Spot Inflection Points in Business Before They Happen*. Mariner Books.

4. Maxmen, Amy. (2021). *Why did the world's pandemic warning system fail when COVID hit?* Nature. https://www.nature.com/ articles/d41586-021-00162-4

5. Barr, Stacey. (2016). *Prove It!: How to Create a High-Performance Culture and Measurable Success*. Wiley.

6. Pfeffer, Jeffrey, & Sutton, Robert I. (2006). *Hard Facts, Dangerous Half-Truths, and Total Nonsense*. Harvard Business Review.

Chapter Fifteen

1. Bean, Randy. (2021). *Fail Fast, Learn Faster - Lessons in Data-Driven Leadership in an Age of Disruption, Big Data, and AI*. Wiley.

2. Eckerson, Wayne. (2012). *Secrets of Analytical Leaders: Insights from Information Insiders*. Technics Publications, LLC.

3. Trevor, Jonathan, & Varcoe, Barry. (2016). *A Simple Way to Test Your Company's Strategic Alignment*. Harvard Business Review. https://hbr.org/2016/05/a-simple-way-to-test-your-companys-strategic-alignment

4. Lafley, A. G., & Martin, Roger L. (2013). *Playing to Win: How Strategy Really Works*. Harvard Business Review.

5. Jackson, Peter, & Carruthers, Caroline. (2019). *Data Driven Business Transformation - How to Disrupt, Innovate and Stay Ahead of the Competition*. Wiley.

6. Aas, Tor Helge, & Breunig, Karl Joachim. (2017). Conceptualizing innovation capabilities: A contingency perspective. *Journal of Entrepreneurship, Management and Innovation, 13*(1).

7. Lawlor, Patrick, O'Donoghue, Adrian, Wafer, Brendan, & Commins, Eddie. (2015). *Design-Driven Innovation: Why it Matters for SME Competitiveness*.

Conclusion

1. Pearl, Judea, & Mackenzie, Dana. (2020). *The Book of Why: The New Science of Cause and Effect*. Basic Books.

Index

Ingram Content Group UK Ltd.
Milton Keynes UK
UKHW011944180423
420354UK00003B/46